If You Really Trust Me,

Why Can't I Stay Out Later?

If You Really Trust Me,
Why Can't I Stay Out Later?

LORRAINE PETERSON

BETHANY HOUSE PUBLISHERS
MINNEAPOLIS, MINNESOTA 55438

Illustrations by Hugo Rangel

Published by Bethany House Publishers
A Ministry of Bethany Fellowship, Inc.
6820 Auto Club Road, Minneapolis, Minnesota 55438

Printed in the United States of America

Library of Congress Cataloging-in-Publication Data

Peterson, Lorraine.
    If you really trust me, why can't I stay out later? / Lorraine Peterson.
      p. cm.
    Summary: A collection of devotional readings based on the wisdom of Solomon as expressed in the Book of Proverbs.

    1. Youth—Prayer-books and devotions—English. 2. Bible. O.T. Prov-erbs—Devotional literature. 3. Bible. O.T. Proverbs—Use—Juvenile litera-ture. [1. Bible. O.T. Proverbs—Meditations. 2. Prayer books and devotions. 3. Christian life.] I. Title.
BV4850.P462 1991
242'.63—dc20   91-22923
ISBN 1-55661-212-5   CIP
                                                    AC

Acknowledgments

"Every book is a miracle." The statement isn't original with me, but I agree with it totally. If I couldn't rely on the One "who is able to do immeasurably more than all we ask or imagine, according to his power that is at work within us," I could not author a book at all. When I feel that I have nothing worthwhile to say, God gives me new inspiration. When my body and mind rebel against the rigid discipline that writing requires, He provides physical stamina and the ability to concentrate. This manuscript was possible only because of God's mercy and the gifts He has graciously given me.

God also supplies help in human form. Researching this book, I found needed information in the following volumes: *The New Age Cult; Proverbs: A Commentary on an Ancient Book of Timeless Advice,* and *The Bethany Parallel Commentary on the Old Testament.* My editor, David Hazard, has given me many valuable suggestions; the touch of his talent is always evident when my books appear in final form. Another, who works hard behind the scenes, is Carol Johnson, Bethany's editorial director. As I write I also appreciate the constant support and affirmation of my family—my father, my stepmother, my sister Lynn, my brother-in-law Earl, and my nieces and nephews Beth, Brett, Kaari and Kirk.

About the Author

LORRAINE PETERSON was born in Red Wing, Minnesota, grew up on a farm near Ellsworth, Wisconsin, and now resides in Ciudad Juarez. She received her B.A. (in history) from North Park College in Chicago, and has taken summer courses from the University of Minnesota and the University of Mexico in Mexico City.

Lorraine has taught high school and junior high. She has been an advisor to nondenominational Christian clubs in Minneapolis public schools and has taught teenage Bible studies. She has written several bestselling devotional books for teens:

If God Loves Me, Why Can't I Get My Locker Open?
Falling Off Cloud Nine and Other High Places
Why Isn't God Giving Cash Prizes?
Real Characters in the Making
Dying of Embarrassment & Living to Tell About It
Anybody Can Be Cool, But Awesome Takes Practice
If the Devil Made You Do It, You Blew It!
Radical Advice From the Ultimate Wise Guy
If You Really Trust Me, Why Can't I Stay Out Later?

Contents

There's Something You Need to Know Before You Read This Book!

Solomon's book of Proverbs, like Jesus' Sermon on the Mount, explains how you are to behave. It promises blessings for those who live by God's principles and hard times for those who disobey them. Here are some proverbs that explain the benefit of right action and the bad consequences of doing wrong.

A gentle answer turns away wrath, but a harsh word stirs up anger (Proverbs 15:1).

A kind man benefits himself, but a cruel man brings trouble on himself (Proverbs 11:17).

He who scorns instruction will pay for it, but he who respects a command is rewarded (Proverbs 13:13).

He who ignores discipline comes to poverty and shame, but

whoever heeds correction is honored (Proverbs 13:18).

The house of the righteous contains great treasure, but the income of the wicked brings them trouble (Proverbs 15:6).

An evil man is snared by his own sin, but a righteous one can sing and be glad (Proverbs 29:6).

The wicked man flees though no one pursues, but the righteous are as bold as a lion (Proverbs 28:1).

The light of the righteous shines brightly, but the lamp of the wicked is snuffed out (Proverbs 13:9).

When justice is done, it brings joy to the righteous but terror to evildoers (Proverbs 21:15).

The righteous man is rescued from trouble, and it comes on the wicked instead (Proverbs 11:8).

He who conceals his sins does not prosper, but whoever confesses and renounces them finds mercy (Proverbs 28:13).

And I could make the list longer! These principles are so true that even non-Christians who obey them receive the promised prizes, and Christians who ignore them suffer the consequences. But *trying* to be good all the time without the supernatural power and motivation of the Holy Spirit is a real downer. Unless Jesus lives the Christian life through you, you will be plagued by frustration.

IN ORDER TO JOYFULLY PUT THE PRINCIPLES OF PROVERBS INTO PRACTICE, YOU MUST UNDERSTAND TWO THINGS:

1. *The Rule of Salvation: Grace*
2. *The Rule for Living: Putting grace into practice, which includes receiving the power to obey.*

Ephesians 2:8–10 puts these precepts in perspective: "For it is by grace you have been saved, through faith—and this not from yourselves, it is the gift of God—not by works, so that no one can boast. For we are God's workmanship, created in Christ Jesus to do good works, which God prepared in advance for us to do."

Good works can never save you: Only the blood of Jesus can take away sin. If getting to heaven were a matter of earning brownie points, Jesus would never have had to die on the cross. From beginning to end, salvation is a matter of grace—receiving by faith the unearned favor of God.

Some people who accept Jesus by faith make the mistake of trying to follow God's commands in their own strength. But that's a little like vacuuming the floor without turning on the electricity! (The results aren't too great.) God did not just say, "Okay, I'll save you by my supernatural power—but after that you're on your own." You can plug into His power and receive the motivation and strength to obey God. "The righteous will live by faith" (Romans 1:17). The Bible repeats this principle over and over. Unless you're rightly related to God and put all your trust in Him, studying Proverbs will make you depressed. It will only remind you of what you should do, but you'll feel powerless to put it into practice. You and I *cannot* live up to the standard presented without heavenly help.

ASK YOURSELF TWO QUESTIONS:

1. *Have I, by faith, accepted the grace of God for the salvation of my soul?*

If you've never really invited Jesus to forgive all your sins and take complete control of your life, you can do it now! Pray a prayer something like this: (the words aren't magic—your heart attitude is what counts with God):

> *Dear Jesus, I recognize that I've disobeyed your commandments and that's a sin. Thank you that you've shed your blood to take away that sin. I ask you to forgive me and to cleanse my heart. Come into my life as my master—the one who has the right to tell me what to do. From now on, I plan to receive your power to obey what your Bible tells me is right. I ask you to take charge and change me into the kind of person God wants me to be. Thank you for coming into my life. Amen.*

2. *Am I putting grace into practice and receiving God's supernatural power to obey?*

If you're grinding it out day after day, living a defeated Christian life, there's hope for you—and God's promise of victory! First, you must pay the price of surrendering your will totally to God. Give Him everything. Then stick so close to Him and spend so much time with Him that you absorb His resurrection power and His enthusiasm for doing right. When you care more about what God says than what the kids at school think, your life will change. When obeying God is more important to you than pleasure or comfort, you'll discover God's power to overcome weakness and fear. Totally giving your life to Jesus makes Christianity exciting. Peter describes that kind of life: "Who is going to harm you if you are eager to do good? But even if you should suffer for what is right, you are blessed" (1 Peter 3:13, 14).

Once you start putting the principle of grace—receiving from God *everything* you don't have—into practice, you'll never live any other way!

Part One

And the Good Guys Always Win—Heavenly Scoreboard Posts Final Results

CHAPTER 1

Worth Waiting For

The tension mounted. Every eye was glued to the basketball court. Only one shot was needed to end the sudden death overtime and win the tournament. In a daring fast break, the ball was passed downcourt to Jefferson's star center who hooked it in for two big points!

Pandemonium broke loose: Jefferson High would be going to the *state tournament!*

Aware that the T.V. cameras were focused on the band, Scott put his trombone to his mouth to play the school song. But even this magic moment could not fully tear his thoughts away from the crisis in his family . . . from the hospital bed where his mother was fighting for her life . . . from the mounting medical bills that placed his family in danger of losing their home . . . from the worries about his little sister who was having a hard time coping.

At the moment, Scott would have felt more comfortable on the side of the losers. He had to be the only unhappy Jefferson student in the gymnasium. *Where is God?* he wondered. *Is it worth living right? Are Christians really better off than non-Christians?* What was happening to him and his family just didn't seem fair.

That night, alone in his room, tears rolled freely down his cheeks. He needed someone to talk to. He thought of waking his dad—but he already had more than he could handle.

Instead, Scott turned to God with his doubts. "God, it's just not fair that my good Christian family has to suffer so much," he complained. As a matter of habit, he reached for his Bible and flipped it open. In a moment, an underlined verse caught his eye: "The righteous cry out, and the Lord hears them; he delivers them from all their troubles" (Psalm 34:17). Reading on, he found this thought em-

17

phasized: "A righteous man may have *many* troubles, but the Lord delivers him from them *all*" (Psalm 34:19, author emphasis).

That night Scott saw two things: First, God didn't promise that the righteous would never suffer—but He gave His word that He'd deliver us. Second, He doesn't tell us when or how He'll help us escape—but He pledges to lead us. All we need to do is trust Him enough to follow Him to an exit.

Scott thought of Job. He didn't know how long Job suffered, but he remembered his Sunday school teacher saying, "Job's faith in God really paid off. Afterward the Lord gave him twice as much as he had before." That night, Scott knelt by his bed and made a decision: He would trust God no matter what.

➡ ➡ ➡ THIS WAY OUT ➡ ➡ ➡

Asking God to Meet Legitimate Needs

In spite of the instant-gratification, pleasure-at-any-price conditioning of our society, a problem-free life is *not* one of your basic needs. Relying on God and aligning your life with His principles so you can make it through the tunnel of trial *is* absolutely essential.

Realize that God permits suffering for a number of reasons—including: pinpointing unconfessed sin, exposing misplaced priorities, uncovering pride, and forcing us into a closer dependence on Him. Your response should include self-examination, repentance, trusting God to resolve the situation, and standing firm against satanic attack.

Dear God, things are tough right now. _____ and _____ are my biggest problems. I know you're there even if I don't feel your presence and I choose to put my trust in you. Show me if I have sin in my life. Help me see my pride. Guide me as I rearrange my priorities so I can spend more time with you. After I get my life in order, teach me how to deflect the arrows the Devil's throwing at me.

☑ Getting the Facts Straight

The righteous man is rescued from trouble, and it comes on the wicked instead (Proverbs 11:8).

A man cannot be established through wickedness, but the righteous cannot be uprooted (Proverbs 12:3).

For though a righteous man falls seven times, he rises again, but the wicked are brought down by calamity (Proverbs 24:16).

1. When trouble comes, your first concern should be to get right with God. Since God's great promises of deliverance apply only to the righteous, be sure that you've not only confessed every sin, but that you are willing to forsake rebellion, pride, disobedience to parents, laziness, and dishonesty.

2. Don't panic with a "how-can-bad-things-happen-to-good-people" approach. The Bible never promises that the righteous will escape trouble, or that nothing will *attempt* to uproot them.

3. Remember that the Bible *does* promise if the righteous continue to follow God during times of testing, God will rescue them in His way, in His time. If you wait until the game is over, true Christians *are* the winners.

God delivers the righteous. This is so evident that we have a saying: "You can't keep a good man down." If you trust God and wait for Him, He'll take you through the trial and you'll be stronger for the experience. When you get close to people who know nothing of living by biblical principles and find out what their lives are really like, you'll encounter an instability and a constant state of crisis. Being good really is good for you, and being bad really is bad for you!

☑ Rethinking the Situation

Five years later, Scott was finishing his senior year in a Christian college. He could hardly believe it. But when "Turn About Weekend" came—the one weekend of the year when girls asked guys for dates—Candy (the most gorgeous girl he'd ever laid eyes on, missionary's daughter, and fantastic Christian) asked him out. He'd secretly admired her since the day she'd registered as a transfer from a junior college. But because half the guys in the school tried to date her, Scott had been afraid to ask her out. Not only was their "Turn About" date a super success, but Candy became his steady girlfriend.

One night as they strolled in the moonlight, Scott asked Candy why she'd chosen him when she had her pick of any guy in the school. She replied, "Because I could see in you a man whose faith has been tested, a maturity that the others don't have. In fact, I've been wondering where it comes from."

Scott thought back to the year his mother died. He remembered his decision to trust God no matter what. He had seen the Lord care for his family time and again. He knew he had a closer relationship with his father and brother and sister than any of his friends.

God had also used the suffering and sorrow he'd endured for the good of others. When a guy from his church got mad at God because his father had died of a heart attack, the Lord had used Scott to get through to him—and now that friend was studying for the ministry.

Scott returned his thoughts to Candy. He'd never even dreamed of dating anyone so perfect—let alone winning her heartfelt respect! Maybe there was something really big and wonderful starting here! He couldn't help but wonder—what if he'd rebelled against God because of the suffering and loss? Without God where would he be now? What would he be doing if he'd rejected Christianity?

Candy interrupted the silence. "Scott," she spoke softly, "I'm so thankful to God for you. You're the man of God I always dreamed of meeting."

☑ Putting the Truth Into Practice

Are you in the middle of a problem so deep you feel as though there's no way out? Take the following steps:

1. Act like God is smarter than you are, and *trust* Him no matter what.
2. Ask the Lord to show you any unconfessed sin. Repent of that sin and take steps to make the necessary changes in your life.
3. Find a mature Christian with whom you can talk and pray.
4. Don't forget that God does promise to deliver the righteous—but He doesn't promise when. Wait for Him in faith.

CHAPTER 2

Righteousness—The Secret to Success

Tyne felt a little out of place—a stranger in her own country. Because her father was a military officer, they'd been stationed overseas for five years and had only spent one vacation in the States. Maybe things in the U.S. had really changed a lot, or possibly it was that the perspective of a ten-year-old is radically different from that of a girl of fifteen—but Tyne found she had *a lot* of adjusting to do when they returned to the U.S., especially when it came to getting to know her relatives all over again.

For the first time in his military career, Tyne's father was assigned to a base in the Southwest. This meant living relatively close to both sets of grandparents. Many times Tyne had heard her father give his dramatic testimony of being saved and delivered from the dangerous cult his parents were involved in. She'd also listened to her mother recount the many answers to prayer that her family had experienced while she was growing up. But Tyne wasn't quite prepared for the big contrast she saw in her two grandmothers.

First, Tyne and her sister Loralyn spent a week with her mother's parents. Grandmother Price was full of love and acceptance. Although her house was average, it was so carefully decorated that it appeared elegant. She was very interested in all the activities of her granddaughters, and she and Grandfather had exciting things planned for the girls to do. An attitude of contentment, joy, and thankfulness pervaded the house. Devotions after breakfast were fantastic, because these dear older people really knew how to pray. They shared answers to prayer and proudly displayed some gifts and pictures from missionaries they prayed for and helped to support financially. The week went by all too fast.

Warned by their parents not to swallow any false doctrine, Tyne and her sister packed off to visit Grandpa and Grandma Watson. After the first day, the girls realized that complaining would be on the menu for every meal. Grandpa and Grandma Watson kept up a continual harangue about the fact that they had bought their home from a "crooked" real estate firm, which had overcharged them and promised a fantastic recreational center that was never built. Grandpa Watson was bitter. When he got going on the topic, it was easy to see why he suffered from high blood pressure.

Grandma Watson, it seemed, was mad at her sister and hadn't spoken to her for two years. Over and over, she talked about how her sister had married a bum, had six children, and then expected a hand-out when she lost her job. The story always ended with, "She deserves her life. She chose it." Another favorite theme was that friends had deserted her. "It's tough to get old," she would say. "All your friends forsake you."

But even worse was her grandmother's overwhelming fear of getting robbed or attacked. Each outside door had three locks. There were bars on the windows, an electronic surveillance system and a German shepherd watchdog. They wouldn't allow the girls to leave the house for fear that something would happen.

After two days, Tyne decided she couldn't stand it anymore. She was ready to pick up the telephone and tell her mother to come and get them. She knew it would hurt her grandmother's feelings—but who should have to spend a whole week of summer vacation in misery?

➡ ➡ ➡ THIS WAY OUT ➡ ➡ ➡

☞ Asking God to Meet Legitimate Needs

You were born with a need for security. The Devil will always try to rob you of your peace and joy. You must learn to stand against his attempts to do so.

Dear God, Your Word says, "Godliness with contentment is great gain." Help me to make holiness (living according to God's commands) top priority. Show me how to trust You so much that I'm constantly happy and content. Right now, the Devil's trying to get me worried and fearful about _____ . I will obey You and trust that You will work everything out for my good. I receive Your joy, contentment and peace for this day.

☞ Getting the Facts Straight

The wicked man flees though no one pursues, but the righteous are as bold as a lion (Proverbs 28:1).

What the wicked dreads will overtake him; what the righteous desire will be granted (Proverbs 10:24).

An evil man is snared by his own sin, but a righteous one can sing and be glad (Proverbs 29:6).

The house of the righteous contains great treasure, but the income of the wicked brings them trouble (Proverbs 15:6).

As a young person, you get to choose between letting Jesus live His righteous life through you or falling for worldly ways of thinking and living. The stakes are very high—not only in terms of eternal destiny but in quality of life here and now. The older you become, the more your lifestyle will reflect the spiritual choices you've made.

For instance, the person who has a guilty conscience constantly fears being found out. Those who haven't put their confidence in an all-powerful God who protects His own find this planet a pretty frightening place to live. Only Jesus can give you freedom from every kind of fear.

People are also afraid of the future. But with your hand in God's, you can walk into the unknown with the Architect of all your tomorrows by your side. You have nothing to dread, because He is your Friend and He loves you.

If you put God first, He'll supply your every need. Even better, He'll make sure that your possessions give you peace instead of worry, turmoil, and the pressure of working two jobs so you can own even more. Because the person who is obeying God doesn't have to cover one sin with another, or cling to material belongings, he or she is free—free to sing and rejoice in the Lord, "who richly provides us with everything for our enjoyment" (1 Timothy 6:17).

✔ Rethinking the Situation

Before reaching for the telephone, Tyne decided to have her devotions. She read Proverbs 11:23: "The desire of the righteous ends only in good, but the hope of the wicked only in wrath." She realized that in her two sets of grandparents she was seeing the real life application of that verse: Grandma Price desired God's will and the result was a tremendous blessing for herself and every person she influenced; Grandma Watson hoped for riches and friendship without being willing to give unselfishly or help anyone else, and therefore she was frustrated.

The whole difference boiled down to this: In one life Jesus was in control; and in the other, existence depended completely on *self*. How could she expect Grandma and Grandpa Watson to be any different? They didn't have the supernatural power of Jesus to draw upon. They didn't even have the right biblical rules to live by.

Suddenly she felt a great compassion for her grandparents. Because she'd always accepted as fact that her father's parents weren't Christians, she'd never consistently prayed that they'd come to know Jesus. But now she saw firsthand how completely lost they really were!

"Loralyn," she said to her sister, "Grandpa and Grandma Watson are missing out on everything good in life. It's our job to pray that they'll accept Jesus. Let's ask God to show them their need of a Savior."

Each night, they faithfully prayed for their grandparents' salvation. On the last day of their stay Grandma Watson remarked, "You girls are so secure and content. I'd like to know your secret."

✔ Putting the Truth Into Practice

Using a concordance, look up all the verses in Proverbs that use the word *righteous* and the word *wicked*. Make a list of the qualities and consequences of both righteousness and wickedness. Seeing the contrast should lead you to two decisions:

1. I determine to live in righteousness and holiness all my life.
2. I must receive power from the Holy Spirit to witness to the non-Christians I come in contact with.

Let Jesus give you His compassion, even for the evil people who are messing up the world. Pray for their salvation. Make winning the lost your top priority.

CHAPTER 3

"Living It Up" Can Be a Real Downer

It was a gorgeous fall day—but as Kayla walked home from school she couldn't appreciate the spectacular red oaks that lined the boulevard, or the brilliant oranges and yellows of her mother's chrysanthemums lining the front walk. She was still too embarrassed to think straight. "How could I have said anything so dumb?" she berated herself.

Painfully Kayla relived what had happened during lunch. Jenna had announced to everyone at the table that she was madly in love with someone named Isaac something. Hearing the name meant nothing to Kayla and she asked innocently, "Does he go to our school?" Uproarious laughter followed. "Are you sure you're a resident of planet earth?" asked one girl. "I can't believe you're for real," quipped another. "He's a rock star—where have you been?"

Kayla *knew* the story would spread throughout the school, and she'd be "Nerd of the Year."

Raised in a sheltered Christian environment, Kayla had attended Christian schools until her father lost his job and was unable to pay her tuition. Because her parents kept the radio dial tuned to Christian stations and carefully monitored T.V. programs, Kayla had little contact with "worldliness."

Registering for tenth grade at Central High had changed all that. She'd been totally unprepared for her new environment, and today's blunder made her feel like a foreign exchange student struggling to survive in an alien culture. She was completely out of it.

In a short time, though, Kayla's attitude changed. Everyone else seemed to be having a lot of fun, and Kayla began to envy the kids at school. For the first time in her life she let herself have doubts about Christianity. Neither heaven nor hell seemed important to her at that moment. After all, she was young and maybe she needed to live it up. Maybe she was missing out on a whole lot—and the comments of other students seemed to prove it: "The party was a blast." "You haven't lived until you've gotten high." "Going out parking with Rick makes my weekend."

Kayla decided to fit in.

She learned quickly and began living a double life: model Christian daughter when her parents were around, and fast-lane chick at school. She was invited to the right parties and did all the in things.

Then Vince, the class president, broke up with Lindsay, the self-appointed leader of the most prestigious girls' clique, to date Kayla. The fireworks began. The entire group had stopped speaking to Kayla.

Kayla had thought that dating a popular and handsome guy would make her feel accepted. Instead of the moonlight-and-roses romance she had dreamed of, Vince bossed her around a lot and made fun of her. She was afraid to ride with Vince when he'd been drinking, and he kept pressuring her to have sex with him—just as if it were no big deal. And then she heard the horrible rumor that was spreading: Kayla had had an abortion.

Kayla got up enough courage to admit to herself that she was now more miserable than ever. Compromising her Christian standards had brought neither popularity nor happiness.

▼ ▼ ▼ THIS WAY OUT ▼ ▼ ▼

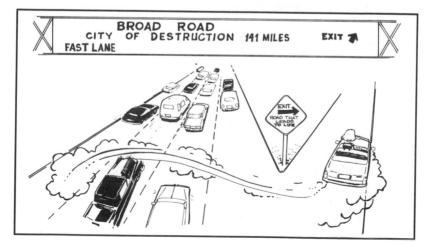

✓ Asking God to Meet Legitimate Needs

Dear God, when I'm tempted to envy the wicked, give me the discernment to see that worldly fun ends in disappointment— and that "you will fill me with joy in your presence, with eternal pleasures at your right hand" (Psalm 16:11). I receive from your Holy Spirit the power to stand alone when necessary. Make me secure in you so I don't fall for Satan's lie that the admiration of my peers determines my value. I know that your love and your approval give me eternal worth. Supply my need for Christian friends, human affirmation, and a healthy, Christ-honoring social life.

✓ Getting the Facts Straight

What the wicked dreads will overtake him; what the righteous desire will be granted. When the storm has swept by, the wicked are gone, but the righteous stand firm forever (Proverbs 10:24, 25).

Do not envy wicked men, do not desire their company; for their hearts plot violence, and their lips talk about making trouble (Proverbs 24:1, 2).

Do not let your heart envy sinners, but always be zealous for the fear of the Lord (Proverbs 23:17).

Do not be deceived: God cannot be mocked. A man reaps what he sows (Galatians 6:7).

The Devil has a well-designed strategy to make wrongdoing look attractive. Often he starts by getting you to look up to some rock star or some loose-living, popular kid. His tactics for getting you to envy the wicked and attempt to copy them will include some combination of the following:

1. The *mirage* that sin is fun, maintained in part by either over-stimulating emotions (bright lights, loud music, hyperactivity, sex) or by dulling the senses (alcohol, drugs, Eastern meditation) to the point that the person can never take time out to think things through.
2. Satan's big lie that being good is bad for you—abnormal, drab, and dismal—that people who do what's right don't enjoy life. (And if you're not depending on the Holy Spirit's inexhaustible

power, available to every born-again Christian, choosing right can be agony.)

3. Not showing you how the movie ends (AIDS, addiction, suicide) and selecting little sections that look appealing.

The Devil plays on a young person's tendency to look at things by the day, not by the year or by the decade. Right this minute, the guy who uses cocaine and brags about his sexual conquests may seem happier than you are—but don't let this carry you to the illogical conclusion that it "proves" non-believers have more fun than Christians. Just remember that Moses, who "chose to be mistreated along with the people of God rather than to enjoy the pleasures of sin for a short time" (Hebrews 11:25), would have told any Red Sea reporter that following God was worth it.

When you're tempted to fit in with the crowd because you don't see any present benefits for being good, remember that God doesn't give a time limit for fulfilling the desire of the righteous, and for seeing to it that the wicked receives what he fears most.

Rethinking the Situation

Kayla was sitting on a park bench across from school waiting for Vince to finish basketball practice. She was trying to decide whether or not to break up with him. Their relationship wasn't meeting her expectations—but since the nasty rumor had turned all the girls against her, she didn't think she could stand being totally isolated.

Lost in her confusing thoughts, Kayla was startled by a sudden presence. "Mind if I sit down by you for a minute?" asked Pam, a girl Kayla had ignored because she didn't travel in the "right" crowd.

Kayla shrugged.

"I just noticed that you seemed a little sad," Pam began. "I'm not quite sure how to say this so you'll understand—but I've given my heart to Jesus. When I have problems I can just go to Him in prayer."

"Oh, I'm a Christian, too," Kayla interrupted. "I transferred here from Faith Academy." When she saw the shocked expression on Pam's face, she added, "I know I don't *act* like a Christian at school, but I just can't handle the peer pressure."

"I used to constantly worry about what the other kids thought," Pam confided. "Then one day I made a decision. I put Jesus' opinion of me in first place. Since then, I've found that if I depend on the Holy Spirit, He gives me the courage I need, the words to say, and the power to swim against the current. Just today, God gave me the strength to present a Christian position during our discussion of the sexual revolution in social studies class. When I tried to be half Christian and half pagan, I was miserable. But living completely for Jesus is great."

Just then Vince drove up. "Are you the chick who ordered a taxi?" he teased.

"I changed my mind," Kayla heard herself say. "Pam and I have something real important to talk about."

◢ Putting the Truth Into Practice

1. Decide never to envy the wicked—even if drug dealers are filthy rich, "Miss Immorality" has all the dates with the cute guys, and "Marty the Mouth" hasn't stayed home sick since first grade. Wait until the movie ends. "How suddenly are [the wicked] destroyed, completely swept away by terrors" (Psalm 73:19).

2. Decide to break the tyranny of peer pressure by putting Jesus' opinion above that of your friends. Get your security from the One who will never leave you or forsake you.

3. Receive from the Holy Spirit all the power you need for overcoming. An in-depth Bible study of Romans 6 and 8 could help you. (I'd also suggest *The Eagle Story*, available from Institute in Basic Youth Conflicts, Oakbrook, Illinois 60521.)

CHAPTER 4

Righteousness Is More Than Skin Deep

When Dave moved to Pinesville, he became Kyle's best friend almost automatically. Their parents were constantly together, they attended the same little church, they played on the varsity basketball team, and as seniors in a small school, they shared every class except one.

Kyle had a certain charisma about him that made him a sensation wherever he went. He was always chosen captain, president, or leader. Very quickly Dave started to feel like his shadow—seldom noticed and *never* the main attraction.

Kyle was the first to give a testimony at church, quick to witness to kids at school, a top student and the president of the senior class. Most kids at Pinesville High expected their leaders to excel and to have high moral standards, so except for a few rebels everybody looked up to Kyle.

Now and then, however, Dave was shocked at Kyle—an off-color joke in the locker room, a date with Heather whose reputation was far from spotless, and the time he cheated on the physics exam. But his charm, apparent sincerity, and obvious success made Dave look past his faults.

It was a foregone conclusion that the two of them would room together when they both started at the University of Minnesota. The first week was great, but then Dave realized that Kyle was living a double life. When he was with students from the Christian group on campus, he couldn't act more spiritual. But he also went out with the guys from the dorm and got drunk, and started dating the loosest girl on campus.

One Thursday afternoon, while both of them were in the room studying for Friday's big exam, their pastor unexpectedly appeared at the door. Dave could tell from the look on his face that something was wrong. "Boys," he said with a pained expression, "I have something to tell you. There was a terrible car accident. Your fathers were driving to Duluth. A truck hit them head on—and they were both killed instantly."

Too stunned to speak, the dazed boys began packing their suitcases to leave, while the pastor made all the necessary arrangements with the university authorities.

It was like a nightmare. The three of them rode for miles in complete silence. Finally Kyle blurted out, "It's not fair! My father was a good man. It's not worth being good. I know lots of guys who do drugs and steal, but their dads are alive!"

Dave continued to operate in a fog—trying to be strong to support his mother and sister, making funeral arrangements, digesting the long list of "never agains," and receiving everybody's sympathy. All the while, he wrestled with the problem Kyle had voiced: "Why?"

When they returned to the university, Kyle made it clear that he was mad at God. He started drinking heavily and even got into drugs. One night he woke Dave up to tell him his pregnant girlfriend was planning an abortion.

◆ ◆ ◆ THIS WAY OUT ◆ ◆ ◆

BUT THE ROOT OF THE RIGHTEOUS FLOURISHES
PROV. 12:12

☑ **Asking God to Meet Legitimate Needs**

Dear God, I want to be a branch who's always in a right relationship with the Vine. Show me how to permit your righteousness and your goodness to flow through me. I know that my own righteousness is only skin deep. It can't save me, or stand up in a crisis.

☑ Getting the Facts Straight

Whoever trusts in his riches will fall, but the righteous will thrive like a green leaf (Proverbs 11:28).

The fruit of the righteous is a tree of life, and he who wins souls is wise (Proverbs 11:30).

The fear of the Lord is a fountain of life, turning a man from the snares of death (Proverbs 14:27).

Being "saved" includes receiving forgiveness of sins and accepting the righteousness (virtue, goodness, correct behavior) of Jesus. But it's not a whitewash job, designed to fool God into not seeing our sins. It's being correctly connected to the living righteousness of Jesus, which flows through us, flushing out the sinful and the undesirable.

Proverbs compares being righteous to "a fountain of life." We maintain the pipeline by having such high respect for God (the "fear" of the Lord, as Solomon puts it) that we go to Him first, listen only for His commands and principles, and train ourselves to do only what He says. The sin that clogs up the works must be removed by confession and repentance so God's love and power can get through. In short, we learn to let God's life flow *through* us.

The real righteousness that Jesus pours into our lives has an indestructible quality. Because it is a strength from Him, tragedy, turmoil, and trouble cannot stop it from triumphing in the end. Not only will there be victory, there will be good fruit.

When trials come, concentrate on your unbreakable connection to Jesus, not on the problems. The solution depends on your receiving the righteousness of Jesus:

I am the vine; you are the branches. If a man remains in me and I in him, he will bear much fruit; apart from me you can do nothing (John 15:5). . . .blessed is the man who trusts in the Lord, whose confidence is in him. He will be like a tree planted by the water that sends out its roots by the stream. It does not fear when heat comes; its leaves are always green. It has no worries in a year of drought and never fails to bear fruit (Jeremiah 17:7, 8).

☞ Rethinking the Situation

Dave's heart ached for Kyle. All this time he'd been an actor, not a Christian who had learned to receive the forgiveness and strength of Jesus by giving over the control of his life to the Lord. Although Kyle had fooled a lot of people for a long time, his mask was falling off. Dave knew him well enough to realize that, unfortunately, he wasn't yet ready to listen.

The whole situation caused Dave to do some deep thinking. Kyle's anger—because he was "a good guy being treated badly"—had no basis. True righteousness, he realized, isn't doing a bunch of good things; it's being rightly related to Jesus, the Vine. And for the person who truly has the power of Jesus flowing through him, transforming the difficult into an opportunity to experience more of the grace of God, there is no place for bitterness.

Dave compared his situation to Kyle's. Because Dave had chosen to receive from God, he'd grown spiritually as a result of the tragedy, and he'd had opportunities to witness, which resulted in leading three people to Christ. His family had grown even closer together. His habit of having daily devotions had paid big dividends. Nearly every day God highlighted a special verse, tailor-made for his needs. He learned to receive the love and comfort of Jesus as never before.

One day he read, "Righteousness delivers from death" (Proverbs 11:4). At first, he was tempted to become angry. But then he opened his heart to God, and felt God's compassion for his hurt and confusion. And along with that came a realization: He knew that his Christian father had passed into the presence of Jesus—a literal deliverance from death. And in a very real way, his receiving the righteousness of Jesus was also delivering him from the *sting* of his father's death. His Christian friends were standing by him while Kyle's drinking buddies could care less. He received encouragement from God every day, while Kyle became more and more bitter. Although it was still hard, he could enter into happy events again, while Kyle was still depressed and had gotten himself into serious trouble.

Two months later, Kyle interrupted Dave's studies. "I don't see how you do it," he conceded. "Your dad was killed, too. You were able to get on with your life—and I've even thought about suicide. I don't know what my problem is."

"Kyle," Dave leveled with him, "you've been playing a part, doing what's 'expected' of you, and relying on your own righteousness. You need to know how to get into a right relationship with the Vine. Then the supernatural life that flows from Jesus will change you from the inside out."

And that night Kyle exchanged the chains that pride and rebellion had constructed, and accepted the freedom of new life in Jesus.

☑ Putting the Truth Into Practice

1. Read John 15:1–17.
2. List all the commands.
3. Read Galatians 5:22, 23. List the fruit you'll produce if you really remain in Christ.
4. Notice that no trial or problem can interrupt this process of your remaining in Christ and receiving from the Vine the power to bear fruit—unless you leave Jesus to become preoccupied with your circumstances.
5. Decide to concentrate on being rightly connected to the Vine, not on frantic activity, endless introspection, or concern for what's happening around you.

CHAPTER 5

Where the Rubber Meets the Road

Trent and Patrick had been friends since fourth grade. Although collecting the most baseball cards and skateboarding to the beach were only memories, they still had common interests—sports, fishing and "intellectual" discussions. Yet in some ways they were very different.

Trent thought things through carefully before making decisions, while Patrick was spontaneous—and sometimes pretty foolish. Trent had always invited Patrick to church with him, but Patrick was a "chameleon Christian"—one who found it easy to change colors to fit in with any crowd. Moreover, because he darted from one thing to another, his life lacked direction.

Then Patrick and his family started attending New Age, *self-actualization* seminars, and Patrick absorbed the new teaching like a sponge. He talked about every person being "part of God." He proclaimed that evil didn't exist, and declared that each person could create his own "reality." He was all excited about learning to contact the spirit world and manipulating "natural forces" to increase his personal power.

Alarmed, Trent began studying his Bible more so he could explain to Patrick why New Age thinking was dangerous. But somehow their conversations were always interrupted. Finally, Trent invited Patrick to go fishing and prayed that he could talk some sense into him. He met with his youth pastor to get some of his own questions answered and to write down the Bible references he'd need to help Patrick. He'd asked his family and friends to pray for him and he brought his Bible along with his fishing tackle.

While they were eating lunch, Trent told Patrick, "I'm really worried about you. You need to stay away from most of those things you're getting in that seminar.

"Please don't get into channeling," he pleaded. "If you contact the supernatural, you'll be talking with demons. That's why God says here in Leviticus 20:6, 'I will set my face against the person who turns to mediums and spiritists.' And the law of Israel says, 'A man or woman who is a medium or spiritist among you must be put to death' " (Leviticus 20:27).

Patrick only laughed. "That's *your* reality," he replied. "I believe we're all part of God and God is in everything, so nothing can be evil. Besides, man is learning so much and evolving so fast that things written a few *years* ago are outdated. And the Bible—well, that's *ancient* history."

"Patrick," Trent agonized, "what do you base your belief on? All your ideas have their roots in Hinduism. I'd hardly consider India a model of a great spiritual society."

"That's your point of view and you're welcome to it," Patrick replied amiably. "I'm seeking more power and a better life. My feelings tell me that I'm on the right track."

"But Patrick," Trent replied in desperation, "don't you believe that some things are true and others are false? Can't you tell right from wrong?"

When Patrick shrugged, Trent remained silent. But he just couldn't understand how Patrick could swallow such thinking without even questioning its origin.

✦ ✦ ✦ THIS WAY OUT ✦ ✦ ✦

☑ Asking God to Meet Legitimate Needs

Knowing the truth and the rules on which God has built the universe so you can live in harmony with them is essential for your well-being and happiness. You need the indwelling power of the Holy Spirit, so He can "guide you into all the truth" as you study the Bible, and receive His power to obey God's Word.

Dear God, lately I've been wondering about _____ and _____ . Show me what I should believe and what is the right thing to do. I will look for the answers in your Word.

☑ Getting the Facts Straight

The wisdom of the prudent is to give thought to their ways, but the folly of fools is deception (Proverbs 14:8).

Righteousness guards the man of integrity, but wickedness overthrows the sinner (Proverbs 13:6).

A simple man believes anything, but a prudent man gives thoughts to his steps (Proverbs 14:15).

The simple inherit folly, but the prudent are crowned with knowledge (Proverbs 14:18).

The sloppy thinking that accepts everything with the openmindedness of a garbage can has nothing to do with biblical Christianity. The apostle Paul didn't go around asking people to relax so they could experience spiritual phenomena. "He reasoned with them from the Scriptures, explaining and proving that the Christ had to suffer and rise from the dead" (Acts 17:2, 3). Historic Christianity is based on the fact that God the Creator exists and has revealed himself to man through His Son Jesus Christ and through the Bible. You can know what *He's* like, find out what *He* requires for salvation, and live by *His* rules. When you live within the bounds He has set, your life is filled with blessing.

Accepting everything as good and part of God means that "truth" includes thousands of contradictions. "Creating your own reality" implies that you are a god greater than the One who made the universe, since you can create reality and He can't! Relaxing, meditating, or going into a trance to eliminate doing any hard thinking is both dangerous and dumb.

It is *not* true that God doesn't care how you express your love to

Him, as some false teachers claim. John 4:24 says, "God is spirit, and his worshipers must worship in spirit and in truth." God requires truth. It's not okay with Him if you worship Him by serving your friends poisoned Kool-Aid, by making an idol, or by taking drugs to expand your mind.

Don't be a simpleton or a fool. Don't believe *anything* unless it lines up with the Bible. Do your homework. Check out different topics with a Bible concordance. When you don't know the answers, ask a mature Christian who has studied the Bible more than you have. Christianity is based on *fact*, not on feeling.

Rethinking the Situation

Trent came home defeated and disappointed. "I didn't even get to first base," he told his mother. "Patrick is off in a fog. To him, nothing is true and nothing is false. According to him, I'm not wrong and neither is he—even though we believe opposite things. Whether or not a society can function on his beliefs just doesn't matter. If I started worshiping jelly beans, Patrick would say that he couldn't judge my truth!"

"Trent," his mother reminded him, "you're just responsible for *presenting* the truth. Only the Holy Spirit can convict someone of sin. You pray for Patrick, God will do the work."

Although Trent knew his mother was right, it was hard for him to resist the urge to say something or do something drastic to wake Patrick up. But instead, he kept on praying.

One day, Patrick came to school really upset. He had just cashed his paycheck before attending his seminar—and during the meeting someone snatched his wallet from his jacket pocket. When he complained to his leader, he was told that it must be part of his *karma* and that he was being punished for something he'd done in a former life. "Stealing isn't evil for everybody," the leader had explained calmly. "Maybe it was right for the person who took it. Since we're all part of God, it is impossible to pass judgment on any action."

"Trent, I guess you're right," Patrick conceded. "When the rubber meets the road this philosophy doesn't make sense. That money was mine. I worked for it, and I have a right to it."

Trent could see that Patrick was now ready to listen, and he thanked God for answering prayer.

✓ Putting the Truth Into Practice

Make a list of things your friends believe. After each one put true or false along with the scriptural evidence.

EXAMPLES:

Reincarnation. FALSE, Hebrews 9:27.

Sex outside of marriage is okay. FALSE, 1 Corinthians 6:9–11, 16–20.

Each person can find God in his or her own way. FALSE, 1 Timothy 2:5; John 14:6.

We are all part of God. FALSE, Isaiah 45:9–12; Psalm 102:25–27.

We can create our own reality. FALSE, Psalm 115:3; Isaiah 43:13.

Nothing can be judged as evil. FALSE, Revelation 21:8; Galatians 5:19–21.

I can work my way to heaven. FALSE, Ephesians 2:8–9; Titus 3:5.

Karma (actions in a previous existence determine your rewards and punishments in this life). FALSE, John 9:1–3; 2 Corinthians 5:17; Hebrews 9:27.

CHAPTER 6

Build Your Bomb Shelter Before the Explosion

When a "For Sale" sign went up on the neighbor's yard, Crystal's mother worried about what kind of people would buy the house. Finally, the sign was taken down, a moving van appeared, and a car with an Alabama license plate was parked in the driveway.

After a couple of days, Crystal's mother took over a plate of cookies to welcome the new family. Crystal and the rest of her family listened eagerly to her Mom's report at the dinner table. Not only were the people Christians, but they had a son exactly Crystal's age.

A week later, Crystal's mom invited the new neighbors over for dinner. Common interests and a mutual ability to see the humorous side of things knit the families together. But Crystal's attention was fixed on Caleb. He had been created exactly according to the recipe—"tall, dark, and handsome." In addition, she found his southern charm completely disarming. As they talked, Crystal discovered that Caleb was planning to be a missionary doctor. And when he asked her if she'd give him a tour of the city in exchange for a stop at Pizza Hut, she enthusiastically agreed.

When they began seeing quite a bit of each other, Crystal knew she was falling in love. Caleb met her expectations in every way. God was first in his life. Although he kept the tone of their relationship very casual and always arranged double dates or group activities, Crystal hung on to each little indication that he might really be serious about her.

Then one day it happened.

"Crystal," Caleb began, "I really enjoy your friendship. You're a fantastic person. It's just that before I moved here, Leanne and I had a very serious relationship. We were told that we should both get to know other people in order to enjoy a full social life and to make sure

41

of how we feel about each other. I can tell that, for you, this is becoming more than a friendship. So I need to be honest with you—I still want to be your friend, but I don't feel it's fair to ask you out again."

Crystal felt hot tears run down her cheeks.

"I'm really sorry," Caleb went on. "I didn't mean to mislead you. I'm not rejecting you. Personally, I'd like to keep on hanging around with you, but I know it would hurt you even more."

Crystal recovered enough to thank Caleb for all the good times. But when she got out of the car, she ran inside the house, went straight to her room, and cried and cried.

▼ ▼ ▼ THIS WAY OUT ▼ ▼ ▼

☛ Asking God to Meet Legitimate Needs

Having everything you want and the assurance that all will turn out exactly as you have dreamed is not a *need*. In fact we "King's Kids" would become impossible, spoiled brats if our every wish were God's command. An all-knowing God relinquishing His sovereignty to satisfy the whims of finite humans would be crazy and dangerous. What we *do* need is the consolation expressed by the psalmist when he said, "You are my hiding place; you will protect me from trouble and surround me with songs of deliverance" (Psalm 32:7).

Dear God, you know that _____ *is my biggest prob-*

lem. Protect me to the point that I sense I'm wrapped in the armor of your love—a love that constantly deflects the enemy's arrows so my spirit doesn't even get hurt. Be my counselor and my help.

✒ Getting the Facts Straight

The name of the Lord is a strong tower; the righteous run to it and are safe (Proverbs 18:10).

He who fears the Lord has a secure fortress, and for his children it will be a refuge (Proverbs 14:26).

The fear of the Lord leads to life: Then one rests content, untouched by trouble (Proverbs 19:23).

When a storm comes up in your life:
1. Remember that you have two options for facing trouble:
   a. You can run to Jesus for strength and comfort, so that the trial literally does not touch your spirit. His miracles can turn tragedy into blessing for the person who never takes his or her eyes off of Jesus.
   b. You can try facing the problem with your own inadequate human resources, resulting in fear, complaining, unforgiveness and bitterness.
2. Decide to confront Satan's darts from a secure position. If you are in a right relationship with God, hiding in His mighty fortress, your prayers can gain back all the territory the Devil has stolen from you. The fear of the Lord eliminates all other fears.

✒ Rethinking the Situation

Since it was only 8:30 P.M., Crystal called the leader of the girls' Bible studies sponsored by the Christian club in their school. Fortunately, Jill was home and said she'd be right over.

Jill listened as Crystal poured out her heart and then hugged her as she cried.

Finally Jill spoke. "God knows the future. You don't. Maybe it's His plan for you to be a famous Christian singer instead of a missionary doctor's wife living in a jungle. You need to trust Him completely for your tomorrows.

"And you need to fall into His arms for the comfort you need. You get to choose whether you'll use God's inexhaustible love and peace, or your own limited strength to meet this crisis in your life. God works miracles. He can show you so much about how to receive His love that you'll be thankful someday that this happened. Don't let the Devil convince you that it's the end of the world and drive you into depression."

After Jill left, Crystal made a decision. She was going to hide out in Jesus' arms. She took out her Bible and read several psalms. They explained exactly how she felt, but they all ended with the hope of receiving God's deliverance. Crystal thanked God ahead of time for her victory.

Crystal's ten minutes a day for devotions stretched to a half hour as she drew closer and closer to Jesus. Instead of feeling sorry for herself on Saturday night when she might have been out with Caleb, she decided to spend a special time with Jesus. His Word became more and more real. She experienced His love and understanding on a level deeper than ever before. As long as she seriously sought after God, she had no time to feel sorry for herself. And her new dimension of faith assured her that God would make no mistakes about her future.

One day, her mother commented, "Crystal, I'm so proud of you. When Caleb broke up with you, I was really worried how you'd take it. I can tell that you've learned the secret that allows God to rescue you from trouble. It's taking refuge in Jesus. Receiving everything you need directly from Jesus helped you through this storm. Remember what you've learned during this tough time, and He'll shield you from many more throughout your life."

☑️ Putting the Truth Into Practice

Sometimes trouble comes in manageable doses—but not always. Sometimes you can form new godly habits that connect you with God during the crisis. But there are things so devastating that trying to acquire new coping skills seems impossible. Don't wait till the bomb falls to try to build your shelter! If you don't learn now to receive love and comfort from Jesus on a daily basis, then if your dad dies, war breaks out, or your best friend betrays you, you'll be too bummed-out to establish new spiritual routines or to make right decisions.

Form that intimate relationship with Jesus *day by day*, so that running into Jesus' arms will be your automatic response when trouble comes.

1. Worship and praise Him in song and by telling Him how wonderful He is.

2. Sit in His presence receiving His love.
3. Memorize Bible verses so you can use "the sword of the Spirit which is the word of God" whenever and wherever you need it.
4. Personalize Scripture and meditate on it day and night—especially as you are falling asleep.
5. Talk over your problems with Him and receive His answers.
6. Read God's Word expecting it to speak to you.

CHAPTER 7

Stopping the Sin Syndrome

Omar didn't notice how dingy and cluttered the back alley was. The rickety stairs that led to his apartment, the back of a corn flakes box that covered the hole in the kitchen window, the leaky faucet, and the legless easy chair propped up with bricks were all part of life as he knew it.

He wasn't surprised to find his father roaring drunk, his mother gone, and the refrigerator empty. But he did try to talk his thirteen-year-old sister out of going to "work the streets" in her provocative sweater and mini-mini-skirt.

"Don't go," he pleaded. "I'll steal whatever you need."

"You'll get caught again," she replied, "and this time they'll put you in jail. I couldn't stand to live here without you. Besides, I'm gonna make some good money, and I'll be back before midnight."

Realizing his arguments were useless, he let her go. Later, he left for the gang's hangout. Walking in, he could see that everyone was already high and that Alex was leading a gang meeting. Impressive gang leader, smart, personable, hotheaded, and an incredible fighter, Alex was already a legend in the inner-city. He was detailing plans for attacking their arch rivals. "We'll all hang around Sanford and Eighth about 7:00 on Tuesday night, and when they show up, we'll make short work of them."

"Your idea is stupid!" Omar shot back. "It won't work. Look at this flyer." He began reading for all to hear, "Citizen Crime Stopper's Meeting—733 Sanford, Tuesday at 7:00 P.M. Program: A panel of policemen to answer your questions."

"If it weren't for Omar, you'd have gotten us all behind bars," D.J. complained.

"And I thought you were so smart," James taunted Alex.

Alex stammered for words. If there was anything he hated, it was being proven wrong. He'd lost face, and everyone could see by his eyes that he was furious. Omar knew he'd gone too far. Now his life was in danger.

Loneliness, desperation, danger, and poverty were all that Omar had ever known. But there was one thing that set him apart from his friends. He was an extremely talented athlete and he lived to play football. The special interest that park board directors and coaches had taken in his life had kept him off drugs and made him a star player in football, basketball and baseball. It also kept him in school.

When Aaron Smith, who had moved from Detroit, showed up for football practice, no one could believe he was for real. Happy, clean-cut and polite, he was such a good quarterback that the newspaper had called him "the high school player whose potential hardly has limits." Aaron took a special interest in Omar and invited him home for dinner.

When Omar entered the door of a modest but immaculately clean apartment, he was impressed by the beautifully set table and the delicious food. It was obvious that the members of the Smith family loved one another and enjoyed being together. He'd never seen a man treat his wife with such respect and tenderness.

After dinner Aaron's father got out the Bible and read from it. Aaron had told Omar that Jesus could change his life, and now he had to admit that Aaron and his family had a quality of life that he knew nothing about.

Omar started spending more time with Aaron. Because they were the two superstars, the football team had an undefeated season going. Determined to win the championship, the coach sometimes held extra long practices. One night Omar and Aaron were the last to leave the field. Hearing footsteps behind them, the boys looked back. There was Alex—with a knife in his hand and a pistol in his pocket. Aaron tried to tackle him but Alex was too quick and stabbed him in the stomach. Attempting to run, Omar was shot in the chest.

THIS WAY OUT

☑ Asking God to Meet Legitimate Needs

Dear God, you know how often I've been tempted to stop swimming upstream and just flow with the current. But I won't because I know you reward the good and punish the bad. Your word says, "He who sows wickedness reaps trouble" (Proverbs 22:8). Help me not to let the Devil convince me that sin is fun and that it has no consequences.

☑ Getting the Facts Straight

When a wicked man dies, his hope perishes; all he expected from his power comes to nothing (Proverbs 11:7).

When wickedness comes, so does contempt, and with shame comes disgrace (Proverbs 18:3).

In the paths of the wicked lie thorns and snares, but he who guards his soul stays far from them (Proverbs 22:5).

He who sows wickedness reaps trouble, and the rod of his fury will be destroyed (Proverbs 22:8).

Sin is the cause of the agony and distress in the world. You will pay a price for your own wrongdoing, and sometimes you'll also suffer because of the sins of society and others around you. Alcoholism, divorce, dishonesty, lack of responsibility, uncontrolled anger and many other actions based on sinful attitudes may hurt you deeply. But by recognizing the root cause of the problem, you can discover the cure.

1. Receive from Jesus *His* power to do right and eliminate the distress caused by your own disobedience to God's commands.

2. Realize that you can break the sin syndrome in your family. First, you can forgive your parents and others who have wronged you. Next, you can receive from Jesus the deliverance and inner healing that can enable you to face life. (Often it is advisable to seek out mature Christian counsel to assist you with this.) Then, with Jesus' help, you can break habits of your own sinful reactions to family members who sin against you. Finally, you can pray in faith that God will save your mother and father and sisters and brothers and change them.

3. Decide to put on your Christian armor to protect you from the sins of others around you.

☛ Rethinking the Situation

After he got out of intensive care, Omar was placed in the same hospital room with Aaron. His father was too drunk to visit him, and his mother had run off with another man. When his sister came, she did nothing but talk about her own problems.

Aaron's family was so different. Cheerful and faithful, they treated Omar as if he were Aaron's brother. They brought cards and presents and kind words. Aaron's father read from the Bible and they always prayed together. Omar could see that Aaron wasn't fretting about not being able to play football. It was obvious that he had forgiven Alex— he even prayed for him! Omar just couldn't understand it.

When Omar was well enough to do some thinking, he told Aaron that he planned to kill Alex as soon as Alex was released from prison. He explained that since his only life's goal—being a football star his senior year—had been shattered, he didn't plan to return to school. "I think I'll hitchhike to California," he decided aloud. "I gotta get away from everything."

"Omar," Aaron instructed, "you need to realize why so many bad things are happening to you so you can do something to break the pattern."

"You mean there's hope?" Omar asked, surprised.

"Sure," replied Aaron. "You can have a good life on earth, and a *forever* in heaven. But it all depends on recognizing sin for the terrible destructive force that it is, rooting it out of *your* life, and asking Jesus to run things for you. The sins of your parents and your sister aren't your fault, even though they cause you suffering. But you can give your life to Jesus and receive His power to stop sin and its terrible consequences in your life. If you have the supernatural power of Jesus to succeed, you'll think twice about getting revenge on Alex and dropping out of school."

"You know," Omar replied, "you and your family are living proof that Jesus can do miracles. You all have the same handicaps I've always blamed for our problems. You're black, you live in a bad neighborhood, you don't have a lot of money or influence, but you dudes are rich in another way. You have love, joy, and peace."

That night, in their hospital room, Omar decided to confess and forsake his sin and give his life to Jesus. Something told him he was breaking the sin syndrome, and finding hope for the future.

Putting the Truth Into Practice

1. Decide to look at sin as your worst enemy and stay as far away from it as possible.
2. List as many consequences of sin as you can think of. Do you really want any of these in your life?
3. Put Psalm 119:11: "I have hidden your word in my heart that I might not sin against you" into practice. Memorize verses that will build fortresses in your life against certain sins, like gossip, lust, laziness, and dishonesty.
4. Forgive those whose sin has caused you suffering.

CHAPTER 8

Even Ms. Bradshaw Can't Obstruct God's Justice!

Shaneill looked forward to her senior year. Most of the twenty-eight members of her class had known one another since grade school. There was an atmosphere of friendliness, respect, and tolerance that permitted Shaneill and the other two Christians to live by different standards and still be considered part of the group.

Shaneill was an honor-roll student who worked hard and respected her teachers. She had always enjoyed good relationships with her instructors, and trusted them to be fair.

But that was before she entered Ms. Bradshaw's senior English class. It was easy to see that this new teacher was extremely nervous and probably had deep personal problems. Shaneill thought that maybe she was having a hard time adjusting to small town living. Ms. Bradshaw was very temperamental and changeable. Picking out certain students as her "teacher's pets," she gave them special privileges.

When the first big exam was given, the TP's (as the rest of the class referred to this group of six) got all the A's. Even Tanya Wilson got an A—probably the first in her entire life. It was rumored that Ms. Bradshaw had invited all of them to her house and given them the answers to the test!

Shaneill was afraid that a B in English would keep her off the honor roll. However, she was totally unprepared for what happened next.

Ms. Bradshaw invited the seniors to a party at her house. Because of her commitment to her youth group, Shaneill respectfully declined the invitation, and so did most of her classmates. When quarter grades were given, Shaneill received a C—the first ever. As shocked students compared grades, it turned out that only those who had attended Ms. Bradshaw's party received A's or B's.

A committee of students went to meet with the principal, but he wouldn't even listen. "Teachers are professionals," he quipped. "If you got bad grades, I'm sure you deserved them."

Shaneill was furious. Usually easygoing and soft-spoken, she became a tiger when injustice was involved. She just expected fair treatment.

Actually, she was too riled up to listen much to her pastor's Wednesday night Bible study, but she did tune in when he said, "If you're depending on someone else rather than God to give you what will make you happy, your trust is misplaced. You may be thinking, 'If only so-and-so would love me, I'd be happy.' Remember that God is love and He has a never-ending supply just for you. Perhaps you're upset over the unfair deal you're receiving. God is just. Look to Him, not to some person for fair treatment."

Wow! thought Shaneill, *I've been expecting justice to come from the principal and Ms. Bradshaw instead of looking to God.* She silently bowed her head and prayed, *Lord, I'm sorry for expecting justice to come from people instead of from You. I know I'm supposed to pray for people in authority over me and I haven't prayed for Ms. Bradshaw even once! Lord, I'm asking You for justice. Thank you for giving it to me.*

▼ ▼ ▼ THIS WAY OUT ▼ ▼ ▼

☞ Asking God to Meet Legitimate Needs

Dear God, I know that you're a God of justice. _____ isn't fair. I ask you to be my lawyer. Protect me and help me.

☛ Getting the Facts Straight

> Fear of man will prove to be a snare, but whoever trusts in the Lord is kept safe. Many seek an audience with a ruler, but it is from the Lord that man gets justice (Proverbs 29:25, 26).

> . . . the Lord, who remains faithful forever, . . . upholds the cause of the oppressed . . . the Lord lifts up those who are bowed down. . . . The Lord watches over the alien and sustains the fatherless and the widow, but he frustrates the ways of the wicked. The Lord reigns forever (Psalm 146:6–10).

> Evil men do not understand justice, but those who seek the Lord understand it fully (Proverbs 28:5).

It's easy to fall into the trap of trying to force those in authority to treat us fairly—and even to give us everything we want. Are you asking God to give your parents wisdom and praying for them every day? Do you accept your mother's no or do you stage a tantrum? When your father says that you can't attend the youth retreat, do you stand and argue or do you pray that God will change his mind?

How often do you ask God to bless your teachers, your principal, and your boss? Pray that they will treat you fairly. There is a time to appeal to them for just treatment, but this should come after lots of prayer and a willingness to accept a negative answer, leaving ultimate justice with God.

Only Christians can really understand justice, because it's based solely on God's principles. God's working out of justice spans both time and eternity. Not all accounts are settled on earth, but we know from the words of Jesus that a main reason that Christians suffer injustice is that they don't pray for God's deliverance. "And will not God bring about justice for his chosen ones, who cry out to him day and night? Will he keep putting them off? I tell you, he will see that they get justice" (Luke 18:7, 8).

☛ Rethinking the Situation

Shaneill returned from a great Christmas vacation determined to study hard for semester finals and get good grades. Making use of some extra time, she'd worked on several paintings for her semester art project.

On the day they were due, she brought them to English class so she wouldn't have to go to her locker between periods. Sylvia wanted to see the watercolors, so Shaneill leaned across the aisle to show them to her. The bell rang, but Ms. Bradshaw hadn't yet entered the classroom. Admiring students gathered around to view the paintings.

Suddenly, the teacher walked through the doorway, snatched the paintings, and screamed for silence. After class, Shaneill humbly went to reclaim her artwork, explaining that she had to turn in her semester project that day. But Ms. Bradshaw refused to give them back, stating that after the bell rang a teacher had the right to confiscate material used to disrupt the class.

Bursting into tears, Shaneill ran to the office and pounded on the principal's locked door. The secretary was so busy she didn't even notice. When Shaneill arrived late for art class, the instructor automatically sent her to the counselor for a tardy pass. Because Mrs. Watkins was out, Shaneill had to wait.

It seemed that there was no one to help her in her moment of need. Collecting her thoughts, she began to pour out her heart to God. She prayed for justice and pleaded with the Lord to help her get her pictures back.

By the time the counselor had returned, Shaneill had recovered her composure and calmly told her story. Mrs. Watkins sent her back to class and promised to try to recover her artwork. The art teacher listened to her with sympathy, but wasn't quite sure what to do. Praying more than she had for a long time, Shaneill got through the day.

As she was putting on her coat to go home, the janitor tapped her on the shoulder. "I found some beautiful paintings with your name on them in the trash," he informed her. "Surely you wouldn't throw away anything so well done!" And he handed her the paintings basically undamaged.

Shaneill smiled with delight, said thank you a dozen times, and ran into the art room exclaiming, "The janitor found them in the garbage!"

Walking home from school, Shaneill thought of how good God was. He knew how to help her when the system was both unfair and ineffective. Now she knew she couldn't count on Ms. Bradshaw for justice, but even she couldn't obstruct *God's* justice. Shaneill began praying about her semester English grade and counting on God's justice.

◤ Putting the Truth Into Practice

Make a list of people who treat you unfairly. Example: (1) My mom makes me do a lot more work around the house than my brother or sister. (2) Kids at school tease me because I have a big nose. (3) The gym teacher constantly yells at me because I'm so uncoordinated.

Decide to pray for these people every day. Memorize Luke 18:7, 8: "And will not God bring about justice for his chosen ones, who cry out to him day and night? Will he keep putting them off? I tell you, he will see that they get justice, and quickly." Using that scripture text as your guide, pray faithfully for God's justice.

CHAPTER 9

Letting God Run the Justice Department

Clusters of lilacs, apple trees in bloom, the lush green of the leaves, and the grass covered with raindrops—it all sparkled in the early morning sun, resembling a multi-dimensional impressionist painting. When Kelly stepped on to this "canvas" to walk across Simpson Memorial Park to her high school, disturbing thoughts kept her from entering into the beauty of a new day. She didn't even hear the special concert rendered by a pair of meadowlarks or appreciate the combination of fragrances that spelled *spring*.

What her father had said at the supper table the night before still upset her: "Mr. Taylor is making my life unbearable," he agonized. "A research chemist should be able to do his job in peace. But because he knows I won't lie to cover up his mismanagement of funds, he's trying to do everything possible to make me quit. I don't know what to do. This is home, and most of our friends and relatives live here. But there's no job alternative for me within a hundred miles."

Kelly's dad was a great man and she loved him very much. He'd worked at Research Laboratories long before Mr. Taylor became executive director. And he'd always enjoyed his work and been well-liked by everyone. It hurt to see how miserable her father was, and the thought of moving scared her. It seemed so unfair that God would allow this dishonest man to cause so much trouble for their family.

Mr. Taylor's daughter, Amanda, was also a junior at Central High. By far the best-dressed girl at school, she'd taken modeling classes. Sophisticated and condescending, she bragged about her dates with the college guys in a neighboring town.

Kelly had tried to be nice to Amanda, but she had a special way of humiliating Kelly. Her snide remarks and insinuations made Kelly feel inferior.

But yesterday had topped everything. A substitute brought a collection of Japanese art to show the students. After their class, several fans were reported missing. When Kelly opened her locker to stash her books before lunch, there were the fans! She brought them to the office immediately and insisted she had no idea how they got in her locker. That was when the principal informed her that Amanda had reported seeing Kelly walk out of classroom with them!

At that point, Kelly was too flustered to think straight. Only later did she remember that Amanda was the principal's office aide and that he was in charge of giving out combination locks to all students. She thought of talking again with the principal—but making an appointment seemed awkward, so she decided to forget it. She kept wondering if he really believed Amanda.

That night, their family attended the midweek service at their church. The Bible study was entitled: "How to Pray for Your Enemies." The pastor explained, "You can pray for God's love in order to love them, because Jesus says, 'Love your enemies.' Pray also for the grace to forgive them, remembering the words of Jesus: 'If you do not forgive men their sins, your Father will not forgive your sins' (Matthew 6:15). And we should pray for justice to be done. Those who oppose us for doing right are God's enemies as well, and we can pray with the psalmist: 'May God arise, may his enemies be scattered; may his foes flee before him' (Psalm 68:1).

"God is in the business of punishing sin and rewarding righteousness *on earth*, as well as in eternity. Taking revenge on anyone is strictly forbidden, because sometimes God sees innocence in a heart that isn't apparent to us. But praying with Jeremiah—'You are always righteous, O Lord, when I bring a case before you'—is well in order. So is echoing the attitude of the apostle Paul, 'Alexander the metalworker did me a great deal of harm. The Lord will repay him for what he has done' " (2 Timothy 4:14).

Kelly had been praying for her dad and for herself, but she had never thought about praying for her enemies or praying for God's justice. That night, Kelly started praying for Amanda and her father. She prayed for the ability to forgive them and love them. She prayed daily that right would triumph. And she found that leaving God completely in control of the justice department gave her a lot more peace of mind.

THIS WAY OUT

☑ Asking God to Meet Legitimate Needs

Dear God, I believe you're just and righteous. I'll wait for you to punish those who sin against me instead of trying to do it myself. _____ has really given me a raw deal and _____ is doing a lot of dishonest things. Give me love-my-enemies love and your power to forgive. I also pray that you'll expose the wrong and protect the innocent.

☑ Getting the Facts Straight

The wicked man earns deceptive wages, but he who sows righteousness reaps a sure reward. The truly righteous man attains life, but he who pursues evil goes to his death (Proverbs 11:18, 19).

Be sure of this: The wicked will not go unpunished, but those who are righteous will go free (Proverbs 11:21).

If the righteous receive their due on earth, how much more the ungodly and the sinner (Proverbs 11:31).

Righteousness guards the man of integrity, but wickedness overthrows the sinner (Proverbs 13:6).

The Devil tries very hard to keep you from believing that God is fair and that you live in a cause-and-effect universe—especially when it comes to morals. AIDS is considered an epidemic that came out of the blue, instead of a disease closely linked to sexual sin. Pregnancy outside of wedlock is largely looked upon as something that just happens, instead of an event over which each teen has personal control—and responsibility. It seems easier to believe in a whatever-will-be-will-be fatalism than to acknowledge that your decisions either make you or break you. But the fact remains that sin is punished and righteousness is rewarded, even in this life.

God "causes His sun to rise on the evil and the good, and sends rain on the righteous and the unrighteous." Hurricanes and tornadoes seem to occur on this basis. But there is a special agony reserved for those who suffer as the result of their own ungodly decisions. The lifelong loss that comes from marrying a non-Christian, attending the funeral of the little girl you hit while driving under the influence of drugs or alcohol, or realizing that you've not only wasted years of your life but you have lead others astray—these things contain a dimension of pain that circumstantial tragedy can't match.

Christians aren't immune to suffering for righteousness' sake, from getting wet when it rains, from dying of old age, or from throwing gutter balls. But their righteousness will guard them from the anguish brought on by sinful decisions. And those who've learned the secret of accepting God's deliverance pass through the deep waters and emerge with a deeper joy and a purer faith.

✔️ Rethinking the Situation

As she entered the stately brick school building, Kelly caught a snatch of a conversation. "I can't believe it," Linda was saying, "a big-time drug dealer living in our town!"

Arriving at her locker she heard Jay ask Dick, "Did you see the morning paper?" Remembering she was late for her appointment with Miss O'Brian concerning her article for the school paper, Kelly started up the stairs, missing Jay's big news. When she entered room 214, Amanda was sobbing her heart out, and Miss O'Brian didn't know how to comfort her.

Because she'd been praying for Amanda every day, Kelly had forgiven her and was genuinely concerned. "Amanda, what's the matter? Is there anything I can do to help you?"

Amanda shoved a tear-stained newspaper at Kelly. The headline read, LOCAL MAN INDICTED BY FBI AGENTS FOR DRUG

TRAFFICKING. Below was Mr. Taylor's picture! The article explained that Mr. Taylor had been involved in importing cocaine from Colombia and selling it in several states.

"Amanda had no idea of her father's activities," Miss O'Brian filled Kelly in. "And she didn't find out about the scandal until she came to school. She thought her father was away on a business trip—and her mother still doesn't know."

"If you can get me excused, I'll walk home with Amanda to break the news to her mother," Kelly offered.

Miss O'Brian nodded. "I'll arrange everything with the office and your teachers."

Managing to duck out the side door, they started walking toward Amanda's gorgeous home. "Amanda," Kelly consoled her, "if you give your heart to Jesus, you can have a good life no matter what."

"Kelly," Amanda began tearfully, "the way you've treated me after the dirty trick I played on you makes me think knowing Jesus really could help me. I'm sorry for putting the fans in your locker. It's no excuse, but my dad said his future depended on getting your family to move out of town. He said he didn't dare fire your dad because he was too popular with members of the board, but that your dad was causing him lots of problems. I guess I got angry, and decided to take it out on you. But my conscience really bothered me."

A few minutes later, they were in Amanda's living room. Staring at the horrible headline, Amanda's mother nearly became hysterical. When she finally calmed down, Kelly explained to both of them how getting to know Jesus personally could give them hope—something to live for. They thanked Kelly and promised to attend church with her on Sunday. Kelly was so grateful she'd learned to pray for her enemies.

When Kelly got home, her father told her that he'd been made executive director of Research Laboratories with a fifty percent raise in pay! Kelly thought, "I shouldn't be so surprised. I know that God is righteous and I prayed for justice to be done."

✔️ Putting the Truth Into Practice

Decide to believe God when He says, "Be sure of this: The wicked will not go unpunished, but those who are righteous will go free" (Proverbs 11:21).

Do the right thing with the confidence that you'll be rewarded for it in the end. Expect God to deliver you from trouble. Look for His miracles that transform suffering into joy, weakness into strength, and uncertainty into faith. God is just. Refuse to listen when the Devil says that God is unfair.

Self-Examination

Part I: And the Good Guys Always Win— Heavenly Scoreboard Posts Final Results

1. When tragedy strikes, what should your response be?
   _____ a. Get things straight between you and God so you can claim all the promises that apply to the righteous.
   _____ b. Don't panic—good people do suffer, but they come out of it victoriously if they continue to trust God.
   _____ c. Wait patiently for God's deliverance.
   _____ d. Tell God exactly how to get you out of this mess.
2. The wicked flees though no one pursues, but the righteous are bold as a _____ (Proverbs 28:1).
3. What method does the Devil use to make sin look like fun?
   _____ a. Overstimulating emotions.

_____ b. Dulling the senses.

_____ c. Spreading the idea that people who do what's right don't enjoy life.

_____ d. Showing the exciting parts of the "movie" without including the sad ending.

4. Being justified by Jesus:

_____ a. Is a whitewash job.

_____ b. Is being rightly connected to the Vine and constantly receiving the life of Jesus.

_____ c. Is like getting water from the Fountain of Life to flush out the sinful and the undesirable.

_____ d. Is letting Jesus pour His righteousness into our lives.

5. Historic Christianity is based on the fact that _____

_____

6. Are you facing a storm in your life? _____
What are you doing about it? _____
Would your situation be improved by some additions or changes in your present action? _____

7. What are some things you personally can do to protect yourself against the damage sin causes?

_____ a. Receive power from Jesus to do right so you won't suffer from your own wrongdoing.

_____ b. Just float along with the crowd.

_____ c. Forgive those who sin against you and pray for them.

_____ d. Wear your Christian armor.

8. Are you being treated unjustly? _____ Are you complaining and trying to force the situation or are you praying for God's justice?_____

9. The wicked will not go _____ , but those who are righteous will go _____ . (Proverbs 11:21).

10. Don't believe anything unless it lines up with _____
_____

Part Two

Honest to God—and to Others

CHAPTER 10

Skipping School—and Learning a Whole Lot

Being a pastor's son wasn't always easy, but Jim played his role well. He earned good grades in school, never got into trouble and showed up every time the church door opened. When his father accepted a pastorate in a large city, Jim found himself in a very permissive school atmosphere. There was no "God Squad" to hang around with. Reading and writing were mostly replaced by rebellion.

Drugs, drinking, and sex didn't really tempt Jim, but he felt so alone. It was like he was condemned to "being good," but he wasn't enjoying it very much. With the advent of spring, skipping school became epidemic—and nobody seemed to get caught.

One morning before the eight o'clock bell rang, a couple of guys from English class invited Jim to cut out with them and eat breakfast at McDonalds. English was the most boring class of the day. Jim felt a little guilty as they snuck out the side door, but he rationalized that he deserved a break. Besides—going out to eat wasn't exactly sin city.

What the three of them didn't know was that in response to a PTA plea, the principal had initiated a new policy. Each student caught skipping would be suspended for one day. When they returned, the school policeman spotted them and escorted them to Mr. Reynolds' office. They were sent home and told to bring their parents with them to be readmitted the next day.

Although Jim felt bad about letting his dad down, his strongest emotion was anger. Why should he get caught the very first time he broke a school rule, when others seemed to get away with murder?

Unlike his friends, Jim knew how to talk with older people and how to appreciate them. Remembering that his folks were out of town for the day, he decided to go have a visit with Mr. White, his seventy-year-old friend who had become like a grandfather to him.

As Jim told Mr. White his problems, he listened with the compassion and wisdom of a man who had walked with God for many years. He didn't say a word until Jim had gotten everything off his chest.

"Jim," he began gently, "there's a reason why being good is so boring for you. Although you accepted the righteousness of Jesus by faith when you were saved, right now you're not walking by faith—not relying on the strength of God. Instead, you're depending on human efforts."

"What do you mean?" Jim interrupted.

Mr. White opened his Bible and began reading from Philippians 2:12, 13: " 'Continue to work out your salvation with fear and trembling, for it is God who works in you to will and to act according to his good purpose.' Because the blood of Jesus washed away your sins, you're justified—just as if you'd never sinned—in God's eyes. He has sent His Holy Spirit to live in you. So if you cooperate with Him and receive His power, being good will become a real adventure.

"You need to begin to realize the great mercy of God in saving you from hell. What a great privilege you have—to be able to draw upon the inexhaustible resources of the power of the Holy Spirit living in you. Then you'll be excited about cooperating with God's work in you to do what's right. Then you'll resist evil because you love Jesus and want to please Him—not because it's expected of you."

▼ ▼ ▼ THIS WAY OUT ▼ ▼ ▼

✔ Asking God to Meet Legitimate Needs

Dear God, I need to see how wonderful your salvation really is, and to be totally aware of your power at work in me. Thank you that you're able to "do immeasurably more than all I ask or imagine according to your power at work within me" (Ephesians 3:20, personalized). Keep me from resorting to my own efforts to try to do what's right, and missing out on the excitement of cooperating with Jesus.

✔ Getting the Facts Straight

The Lord detests the sacrifice of the wicked, but the prayer of the upright pleases him. The Lord detests the way of the wicked, but he loves those who pursue righteousness (Proverbs 15:8–9).

The Lord detests men of perverse heart, but he delights in those whose ways are blameless (Proverbs 11:20).

The Lord detests the thoughts of the wicked, but those of the pure are pleasing to him (Proverbs 15:26).

Nothing is more pleasant than knowing you have the approval of the person you most love and admire. God has provided everything necessary for us to enjoy that kind of relationship with Him!

1. Jesus died on the cross for your sins so you can be cleansed completely if you put your faith in Him. The righteousness of Christ becomes yours.
2. When you accepted Christ, God put within you the dynamite of the Holy Spirit, the same power that raised Jesus from the dead, to enable you to live according to His will.
3. He made you a partner in bringing His righteousness down to earth. Depending on the power of the Holy Spirit and the guidelines found in the Bible, you demonstrate God's right ways of doing things in a crooked and mixed-up world.

✔ Rethinking the Situation

Jim was silent for a moment. He remembered his father's sermon on Galatians 3.

"Mr. White, could I use your Bible for a minute?" Jim asked.

"Sure, here it is," replied Mr. White.

Jim turned to Galatians 3:2–3 and read: "Did you receive the Spirit by observing the law, or by believing what you heard? Are you so foolish? After beginning with the Spirit, are you now trying to attain your goal by human effort?" He also remembered a verse he had memorized as a little boy: "The just shall live by faith."

At last he saw his problem. Although he had accepted Christ, and the dynamic of the *indwelling* of the Holy Spirit was his, he lived his daily life without turning on the "power switch." Instead, he tried to please people, and tried to follow rules and regulations. Because he was accomplishing this by sheer willpower, he was wearing himself out.

Mr. White interrupted his thoughts. "You can learn to trust the Lord and to relax as you obey God's Word, not every rule some person made up. If you blow it like you did today, just ask forgiveness and decide to rely on God's power not to repeat your sin. The more you build an intimate love relationship with Jesus, the more you'll want to please Him.

"Then, instead of living under the pressure to please others, striving to do good and failing, you can build a new sequence: Realizing that you are God's cherished child, you can love Jesus so much that you want to act like Him; then rely on His power to work in you to do what's right; and finally, *enjoy His approval.*"

▶ Putting the Truth Into Practice

Someone has described living by faith as taking the next step even though you don't see another rung on the ladder. And as soon as your foot reaches that point, there is a solid place to stand. I remember how I used to be scared to death to share my faith. Nervous and floundering for words, I'd begin—and God answered that faith by literally taking over the conversation from there on. (He's still performing that miracle for me!)

Take such a step of faith under the direction of the Holy Spirit. Say *no* to friends who are tempting you to drink; stand up for what's right in the class discussion at school; witness to your friend about Jesus; forgive your father; or by faith show love to the person who just hurt you.

CHAPTER 11

Don't Take the "Ostrich Approach" to Truth

Chuck was the office computer aide. When funds were cut and the office staff reduced, top students were selected to take their places and given credit for on-the-job training. Considered absolutely reliable by everyone, Chuck was given the responsibility of feeding report card grades into the computer.

One day Brenda, Mr. Novak's aide, handed him a paper with Mr. Novak's signature, asking the computer room to raise each first-quarter mark given to seniors by one letter grade. Since Mr. Novak was by far the toughest teacher in Park High and hadn't even given *one* A, Chuck was happy to see this humanitarian gesture. Quickly, he changed all the grades.

He soon heard it rumored, however, that some guys on the football team, who had failed, had bribed Brenda to carry out their scheme. Chuck felt uneasy, but justified his lack of further investigation by telling himself that he always had to obey the written instructions of a teacher. He carefully saved the paper in case any questions would be asked.

Confiding in his two closest friends, he was assured that he was doing the right thing. "After all," Craig reasoned, "kids work twice as hard in Mr. Novak's class as they do in any other room, so you've only righted a wrong."

The principal was an easygoing guy, only a year from retirement. He wouldn't make any waves. As the days went by, Chuck felt more comfortable—until Pastor Moore preached a sermon on truth.

"God commands us: 'Stand firm then, with the belt of truth buckled around your waist,' " he thundered. "Truth is the basis for all our Christian armor. And the truth isn't always easy to find. If you adopt an 'ostrich approach' to truth, you'll pay a big price for your ignorance. Often we must search it out. We must pray with David, 'Guide me in your truth and teach me' (Psalm 25:5). Proverbs 23:23 instructs us: 'Buy the truth and do not sell it.'

"A lot of people prefer not to know the truth, because they don't want to change their lives to conform to it. Sometimes one has to do a lot of investigation in order to confirm the facts and thus be able to act correctly. And even then the Devil will try to get us to rationalize, procrastinate—anything to keep us from living by the truth."

Chuck felt convicted. If he presented the paper supposedly signed by Mr. Novak to the office, it wouldn't be hard to find out whether or not it was genuine. But second-quarter grades had already been issued, and if he ratted on Brenda he was afraid of getting beat up by the football players. He convinced himself that his job was to obey orders—not to carry the world on his shoulders. Talking it over with his friends, he again received their stamp of approval for remaining silent.

▼ ▼ ▼ THIS WAY OUT ▼ ▼ ▼

☛ Asking God to Meet Legitimate Needs

Dear God, I know you said, "Then you will know the truth, and the truth will set you free" (John 8:32). I need to know what's right and what's wrong. _____ and _____ are confusing to me. What should I do? I ask you, Holy Spirit, to open your Word to me in such a way as to give me answers for these problems. I will keep looking for the truth until I find it.

✓ Getting the Facts Straight

> Death and Destruction lie open before the Lord—how much more the hearts of men (Proverbs 15:11).

> Who can say, "I have kept my heart pure; I am clean and without sin?" (Proverbs 20:9).

> The lamp of the Lord searches the spirit of a man; it searches out his inmost being (Proverbs 20:27).

> All a man's ways seem right to him, but the Lord weighs the heart (Proverbs 21:2).

> All a man's ways seem innocent to him, but motives are weighed by the Lord (Proverbs 16:2).

> The heart is deceitful above all things and beyond cure. Who can understand it? (Jeremiah 17:9).

God is the only One who can really tell what's in us. It's dangerous to try to determine the state of your own soul. Rationalizing and giving excuses for what we do is normal for all of us. Letting others be our judge causes difficulty and confusion.

The story of Job is basically a dilemma that was made much worse than it really was, because Job insisted that he knew his own heart, and his "friends" were sure that they were the infallible judges of Job's motives. Job was right in refusing to accept the sentence of his "friends," but wrong in assuming he understood what was in his own heart. When Job allowed God to clarify things and admitted, "I spoke of things I did not understand," he was able to repent and gain freedom.

Don't be a slave to public opinion—even Christian public opinion. Don't ever rationalize a verse of scripture. Let the Holy Spirit search your heart and convict you of sin.

✓ Rethinking the Situation

Mr. Thomas was lecturing on Einstein's theory, but Chuck was looking out the window and thinking about skiing. It had been snowing all day, and those big soft snowflakes that were frosting the evergreens across the street were also depositing a layer of powder on the slopes. Then his thoughts were interrupted by a loudspeaker announcement: "Will Chuck Bremmer please report to the principal's office immediately."

Wondering what on earth this was all about, Chuck rose to his feet, walked down the empty hall and entered the office. There he saw Mr. Novak with his gradebook open and an irate mother with two report cards in her hand. "If my Ted really received an F first quarter, why does the computer printout I got yesterday list a D?" she demanded.

The principal turned to Chuck. "You put the grades in the computer. What's your explanation?"

"May I go to my locker to get the paper signed by Mr. Novak which requested me to change the grades?" he asked.

"Certainly," replied the principal.

Seeing the sheet with his forged signature, Mr. Novak hit the ceiling. And when Brenda and the football players who bribed her were called into the office, Mr. Novak's anger boiled out of control.

When the mother accused the principal of incompetence and dishonesty, he completely lost his cool. He suspended Brenda and the football players and then addressed Chuck. "I can't prove your guilt," he stated, still seething, "but I don't think for one minute that you're innocent. I doubt that you really believed Mr. Novak would raise everybody's grade. Brenda did a very good job of forging Mr. Novak's signature, but I suspect you were in on it. We'll have to find another computer aide."

Chuck realized that a lot of kids would also think he was guilty. His failure to seek out the truth had certainly caused a lot of problems. If only he'd listened to the Word of God and the voice of the Holy Spirit instead of rationalizing truth and accepting the values of his friends! The pastor's words came back to him: "Don't take the ostrich approach to truth."

☑ Putting the Truth Into Practice

1. List the things you're into right now that are questionable.
2. After each one, write out the way you rationalize your behavior.
3. As you reread the list, stop at each entry and read this prayer aloud: "Search me, O God, and know my heart; test me and know my anxious thoughts. See if there is any offensive way in me, and lead me in the way everlasting" (Psalm 139:23–24). Stop and listen to the Holy Spirit.
4. Ask the Holy Spirit to bring a scripture to mind for each situation and write it down.
5. Receive from God the strength to take the necessary action to align your life with truth.

CHAPTER 12

The Plight of the "Knight of Right"

Wesley always maintained his Christian testimony while participating in many activities in a public high school—sports, student government, drama, and debate. Because he was a Christian, he didn't tell dirty jokes, he didn't start campaign rumors that would make him more attractive for class office, and he turned down the lead in a play that was less than wholesome. His well-known honesty, submission to authority, and his high moral standards caused his classmates to nickname him the "Knight of Right."

And in real life as well as in fantasy, the good knight had enemies.

Jack, the guy he had beaten out as class president, decided that there must be some way to trap Wesley into wrongdoing. There was something in Jack that just hated the "Knight of Right" and wanted to make him fall.

A series of events warned Wesley that some kind of plot was being launched against him. One night when he opened his history book to study, he found some pornographic pictures strategically placed between pages 101 and 119, the night's reading assignment. He destroyed these without even stopping to look at them. He also noticed that Bridget, wearing even less than usual, kept hanging around his locker and flirting with him. And just before the big chemistry test, Steve offered to give him a "crib sheet" with all the answers. Wesley said *no* to these temptations, and thought that everything was now well under control.

He did have one chink in his armor, however, and he didn't even realize how vulnerable he was. Wesley had grown up in a family where having just the right clothes, buying the best to make an impression, and competing to "keep up with the Joneses" seemed normal. So he wasn't aware of his materialistic hang-up. Money had always come easy and he spent it freely. Now his father's company filed bankruptcy, and the only job he could find was working in a bank—at a third of the salary he'd made previously. Wesley's allowance was eliminated, and he couldn't make much at a part-time job. When a faulty ballpoint pen he'd been carrying in his front pocket leaked black ink all over his good winter jacket he considered it a tragedy.

Accustomed to buying expensive, sharp clothes, Wesley couldn't bring himself to buy the only jacket he could afford—an ugly sale-rack item. A sympathetic clerk came to his rescue. "I'll help you out. If you go buy a store shopping bag, I'll box any jacket you want—no questions asked. No one will ever know."

Wesley struggled with his conscience. Take a jacket without paying for it? He couldn't do that! But instead of praying and leaving the store, he considered his embarrassing situation. Wearing an ink-stained jacket, buying the un-cool one, or freezing to death—each seemed like an unthinkable option. Slowly he walked over and purchased a Dayton's bag. When he returned, he picked out a cool jacket and the clerk boxed it for him. Slipping it into his shopping bag, he headed for the nearest exit.

"Security to door four" he heard over the loudspeaker. And before he knew what was happening, the store detective was demanding to see what was inside his box! Finding no sales slip, he barked, "You're under arrest."

Just then, Janette walked by. "I can't believe you'd shoplift," she chirped. "I thought you were a *Christian*."

▼ ▼ ▼ THIS WAY OUT ▼ ▼ ▼

✔ Asking God to Meet Legitimate Needs

Dear God, you know everything, and you know how strong the fight is between right and wrong. You know that there are kids at school who would love to see me get caught doing something sinful. Help me put my desires under the control of the Holy Spirit so I can resist temptation. Show me how to love good and hate evil.

✔ Getting the Facts Straight

The righteous detest the dishonest; the wicked detest the upright (Proverbs 29:27).

He who leads the upright along an evil path will fall into his own trap, but the blameless will receive a good inheritance (Proverbs 28:10).

Like a muddied spring or a polluted well is a righteous man who gives way to the wicked (Proverbs 25:26).

It would be naive of you not to realize that many of your non-Christian "friends" at school would be delighted if you fell into sin. If Jesus doesn't control a life, then Satan does. His 24-hour, 7-day-a-week agenda is to entice people to do what is wrong. And he'll use a pagan person to influence you whenever possible.

While God has a special punishment for those who "lead the upright along an evil path," the Christian needs to think about the consequences of giving in to the pressure of the wicked. It is true that as soon as you repent, God will give you instant forgiveness. But the figures of speech—"a muddied spring" and a "polluted well"—refer to the state of the testimony of a Christian who lowers his or her standards. It takes a while for the fresh spring water to rinse away all the mud, and even longer to restore a dirty well. In the meantime, its waters spread sickness and poison in the same way that compromising Christians can turn people against following Jesus.

Decide to be a pure and consistent light in the darkness. Then others will follow Jesus because of your good example.

✔ Rethinking the Situation

As the policeman led him out to the squad car, Wesley spotted Jack and his friends running for cover. Among them was the "clerk" who facilitated his theft. After questioning, Wesley was released to the custody of his parents who were very understanding. Wesley confessed his sin to God and he knew he was forgiven. But he dreaded going to school on Monday morning.

It was even worse than he had imagined. Ginny, a sophomore he'd only talked to once, met him at his locker. "Did you really get picked up for shoplifting?" she asked.

"Yes," he answered with shame.

"I'm disappointed in you," she said simply. "I thought I'd at last found a person who lived his Christianity."

Through the grapevine, he heard that Mr. Anderson, the avowed atheist who taught social studies, had spent all hour saying that religious fanatics were all fakes. He concluded that the "Knight of Right," who'd gotten caught shoplifting, was just one more proof.

Even the principal's secretary made a point of telling him, "I never would have thought such a thing of you."

Wesley had no idea that his life was making such an impact. He was prepared for the long uphill climb that would again put him in a position to influence his school for Christ. He would be careful from now on to give every dangerous desire completely to Jesus. Never again would he think, "What I do really doesn't matter."

☑ Putting the Truth Into Practice

1. List your ten greatest desires.
2. Check each one over with Jesus. Is anything out of control? Is there anything you want that is not yielded to God's will?
3. Realize that, as a Christian, you do live in a goldfish bowl. But instead of feeling pressured, receive the power of the Holy Spirit to live in victory.

CHAPTER 13

The Deceitful Dating Dilemma

Danae was the kind of girl you'd look at twice—long, curly red hair, pretty complexion, great figure, and a perfect smile. She was not used to being without a date. But for some reason, nobody had asked her out in weeks.

The thought of attending the church Christmas party with the girls made her depressed. When flirting with the more popular guys at youth club didn't bring the desired results, Danae became desperate.

Finally, she devised a scheme. Ben was painfully shy and somewhat of a nerd. But he was a nice enough guy, and even fairly good-looking. She was sure she could charm him into inviting her to the party, and if things didn't look up she could date him until after the Sweetheart Banquet. In the meantime, she could look for greener pastures.

When she mentioned her plan to Di and Marji, Di told her that she was being dishonest. Marji agreed that it was cruel to deceive Ben into asking her out by pretending she liked him. But Danae's quick sense of humor turned the conversation to other topics, and soon they were giggling together as usual.

Danae asked Ben to help her with her chemistry homework. When he arrived at her house, she looked stunning. Serving hot chocolate and homemade cookies, she acted the perfect hostess. She went heavy on the compliments, and invited him to come over the next evening.

Unwittingly, he came back, and after the homework was completed, Danae asked him to stay for popcorn, cider, and some TV. At just the right moment, she said, "I wish someone as nice as you would invite me to the Christmas party." Ben fell for it.

The night of the party, Ben was so happy and proud to have Danae at his side. He gave her a beautiful pink sweater for Christmas, treated her like a queen, and took her to nice places.

And in February, he invited her to the Sweetheart Banquet, bought her a special corsage, and included a box of chocolates. It was obvious that Ben was crazy about Danae.

But as soon as the Sweetheart Banquet was over, Danae lost interest. She was always too busy to go out and turned out excuses by the dozen.

By this time, Marji was dating David. One day she told him about Danae's trick. David was a good friend of Ben's, so he passed the info along. When Ben showed up at Danae's house demanding to know if the story was true, she didn't want to discuss it and officially broke off the relationship.

Rallying around Ben, the guys from church all gave Danae the cold shoulder. But Danae counted on the citywide youth retreat to produce another boyfriend.

◆ ◆ ◆ THIS WAY OUT ◆ ◆ ◆

✔ Asking God to Meet Legitimate Needs

Dear God, I need to decide that honesty will always be my top priority. It's so easy for me to be sneaky and to plot to get my own way. I know it's wrong. Forgive me for_____

_____
(situation in which you did some manipulating and conniving to get what you wanted)

I acknowledge that not being completely up-front and totally honest is sin.

✔ Getting the Facts Straight

A good man obtains favor from the Lord, but the Lord condemns a crafty man (Proverbs 12:2).

He whose walk is upright fears the Lord, but he whose ways are devious despises him (Proverbs 14:2).

There is deceit in the hearts of those who plot evil, but joy for those who promote peace (Proverbs 12:20).

The integrity of the upright guides them, but the unfaithful are destroyed by their duplicity (Proverbs 11:3).

God is not unaware of the way you treat others. Taking advantage of Chunky Cherry to play a practical joke, manipulating Fred to get your own way, conning Roy into doing your work, or always letting Generous George pick up the bill really makes God displeased with you. He detests any kind of sneakiness or deceitfulness. "The Lord condemns a crafty man" (Proverbs 12:2).

If you decide to be strictly honest—even if it costs you money, even if you lose out on some laughs, even if your friends turn on you—your path will be straight and your life consistent. Besides that, you'll find an inner contentment. Transparent honesty yields peace, while deceitfulness causes problems and strife.

✔ Rethinking the Situation

Danae carefully planned her wardrobe for the citywide retreat. Di's parents drove her and Marji and Di to the lakeside campground. She and her friends arrived just as the spaghetti and French bread were being served. Danae lingered behind her friends hoping to find some handsome hunk to sit by. And sure enough, she spied a vacant seat at the last table next to a tall, blond guy. When she asked if he was saving a seat for someone special, he smiled and said that it was reserved especially for her.

Danae soon discovered that Bryce was a super-sharp guy. His accounts of mountain climbing in Colorado and deep-sea diving in the Gulf of Mexico were fascinating. He explained that he'd only been a Christian a month and that he was really looking forward to the retreat.

Because his parents were agnostics and opposed to his "fanaticism," it was really hard for him at home—but he expected to learn a lot more about living a victorious Christian life from the sermons and seminars.

Danae and Bryce hung around together all day Saturday, and she felt on top again. At last she'd found the kind of guy she was looking for.

But Sunday he avoided her completely. Unable to stand it any longer, Danae went straight to him. "Do you think I'm poison or something?" she asked. "What's with you?"

"The guys from your church told me what you did to Ben," he replied. "I can't respect a person who is intentionally deceitful." With that he walked away.

Danae was heartbroken. But after the final sermon, she realized that it wasn't only Bryce and the guys at church who looked down on evil behavior. God was displeased, too.

After the chapel service she talked to the speaker and tearfully repented for her duplicity. And although it was one of the hardest things she'd ever done, she confessed her sin to Ben and asked him to forgive her.

That day, Danae learned an important lesson: Not only does deceitfulness offend God—it brings its own punishment.

☞ Putting the Truth Into Practice

Take inventory in your own life. When do you use deceit to get what you want? (e.g.—I cry every time my dad says *no*, and usually he changes his mind. Sometimes I say I'm sick just to get out of work.) List specific ways in which you are less than honest in these areas.

1. Manipulating others to get your own way.
2. Using people and taking advantage of them.
3. Getting out of work.
4. Flirting to get attention or to get a member of the opposite sex to do something for you. (This is dishonest because flirting really says, "I'm interested in you romantically." Leading another person on when you don't have the least interest is deceptive.)
5. Using half-truths to pile up evidence for your point of view.

First, ask God to forgive you for the past. With His help determine that you'll be transparently honest in all you do.

CHAPTER 14

The High Cost of Disobedience

Brad's church supported missionaries who ran an orphanage in Mexico. When they came home to tell of their work and show slides, the youth group decided to collect used children's clothing and buy school supplies to send to those cute little kids they saw on the screen. Winter was coming and they could supply these poor children with sweaters, jackets, and socks. Enthusiasm ran high.

Because of his gift for leadership, Brad was put in charge of the project. The youth director had to be out of town for two weeks, and his final instructions to the group were to collect the clothes, wash them, and pack them in the boxes provided. "Don't send anything until I return," he emphasized. "There are special shipping instructions we must follow."

Brad organized the small group to go door-to-door asking for used clothing for kids. When the church young people found out how much work was involved, most of them silently dropped out. But Brad didn't complain. He just did all the extra work himself. He even washed the rest of the clothes when some of the girls went on strike. He figured he was doing this work for God and that a little sacrifice wouldn't hurt him.

The youth director phoned the church to say that he'd be returning a week late, and Brad thought that he'd better just go ahead and send the clothing. "You can't," Sonja declared. "The last thing Wayne told us was, 'Don't send anything until I return.' "

"But Wayne is so laid-back," Brad protested. "He never gets anything accomplished. Winter is nearly here, and the kids need the clothes. I've got the address, and there's nothing so complicated about getting the mailing instructions from the post office."

"Call Wayne before making any decision," Sonja warned. "It's unbiblical to disobey spiritual authorities."

"But in an emergency, a good leader just takes charge. I want to get this project completed. Besides, I don't need to bother Wayne with a phone call when the decision is so obvious."

Without checking, Brad took the boxes to the post office. It was more expensive to send them than he'd imagined. So he emptied the youth group treasury and added $54 of his own—he'd been saving for new running shoes, but he was willing to give up some things to advance God's kingdom. And there was nothing he liked better than bringing a project to a successful conclusion.

▼ ▼ ▼ THIS WAY OUT ▼ ▼ ▼

☑ Asking God to Meet Legitimate Needs

Dear God, because of the way the other kids act at school and the things I see on TV, it's hard for me to take obeying your Word seriously. Even though I know that disobedience to your commands will cause me serious problems, I don't particularly like to obey my parents, work diligently, or control my temper. Right now I'm having trouble obeying you in _____ and _____ . Please help me. I need it a lot. Impress on me the importance of daily obedience.

☞ Getting the Facts Straight

> Listen, my son, and be wise, and keep your heart on the right path (Proverbs 23:19).

> My son, give me your heart and let your eyes keep to my ways (Proverbs 23:26).

> To do what is right and just is more acceptable to the Lord than sacrifice (Proverbs 21:3).

> Does the Lord delight in burnt offerings and sacrifices as much as in obeying the voice of the Lord? To obey is better than sacrifice (1 Samuel 15:22).

When my ninth graders, who were especially talented at manufacturing "Maalox moments," filed into seventh-hour class one Friday afternoon—without making a sound—I *knew* they'd done something wrong. After a couple of brainy kids asked me the answers to the hardest questions on the exam, I realized that someone had stolen a copy of my test. It's human nature to cover up disobedience by good works. And God says that no amount of sacrifice can make up for a rebellious heart bent on doing its own thing.

The Devil peddles his the-end-justifies-the-means mentality everywhere. And again and again he tricks people into believing that if they live good, respectable lives, they have the right to disobey God on one point—marrying a non-Christian, telling a little lie, or laughing at the dirty joke so others won't know they're different. But God demands that every one of His commands be strictly obeyed.

And this is God's standard—not because He's a Big Meany—but because He designed every rule to *protect us* and *help us*. Those who came to Jesus after breaking every commandment can tell you how disobedience to God's principles destroys a life. Don't swallow Satan's lie that obedience is out of style and that freedom without limits is in. You best demonstrate that you love God by obeying Him, and you show that you value your own life by heeding the commandments God gave to protect that life.

☞ Rethinking the Situation

After Wayne returned, he spent a couple of days in his office tying up loose ends. When he came across the shipping instructions given by the missionaries from Mexico, he gave Brad a call. "How are you doing on collecting clothes for the orphans?" he asked.

"We collected enough to fill five extra boxes and I sent it to Mexico over a week ago," Brad answered with pride.

"Brad, how could you?" the youth director moaned. "The last thing I told you was *not* to send it until I returned."

"But it's cold now, and the kids needed the clothes," Brad defended himself.

"Brad, listen to the instructions I received from our missionaries." Wayne's tone was that of controlled anger. *"Don't send the clothes to Mexico.* The mail is very slow and it could take weeks or months for delivery. Besides, customs costs can be very high. Send the boxes to our Texas office. That way delivery will be quick, postage reasonable, and we can use our special-permission letter to bring the stuff into Mexico." Wayne paused, to give the words time to sink in. Then he added, "It's very possible that the orphans will never receive the clothes that you sent.

"Brad," he continued evenly, "I know you well. I'm sure you worked terribly hard on the project. Collecting that many clothes in two weeks is really remarkable. You have a gift for leadership and organization. Besides, you're willing to work hard and to sacrifice. But you're cocky, and very slow to obey orders. You always have a better way of doing things and you don't like being under authority. Maybe this will teach you to listen. Remember, the Bible says, 'To obey is better than sacrifice' " (1 Samuel 15:22).

At first Brad was too stunned to answer. Finally he managed to say, "I'm sorry—I guess I have a lot to learn." After he hung up, he confessed his sin to God and received forgiveness. He decided he'd better stop rationalizing and take God's Word at face value and obey it. Hebrews 13:17, "Obey your leaders and submit to their authority," had taken on new meaning for him.

☛ Putting the Truth Into Practice

1. When is it hardest to obey your parents? _____
_____

2. When is it most difficult to obey your teachers and your boss?
_____

3. Which of God's commandments gives you the biggest problems?
_____

Memorize these verses:
"If you love me, you will obey what I command" (John 14:15).

"Everything that does not come from faith is sin (Romans 14:23).

"I can do everything through him who gives me strength" (Philippians 4:13).

As you go back over your list:

1. Repeat these three verses aloud, and apply each verse to your obedience difficulty.

2. Then apply these facts to each situation:

   a. Obeying God at every point is super-important.

   b. You obey by faith—trusting God to fill your willingness to obey with His power.

   c. Because Christ lives in you and the strength comes from Him, it is possible to obey.

CHAPTER 15

You're the Kind of Person I Like to Do Business With

Melody's father was killed in a car accident when she was six. Although her mom worked hard, she didn't have the training to qualify her for a high-paying job. Making ends meet was a constant problem. But Melody and her brother knew that their mother's love and example of faith was of greater value than a high standard of living.

Melody longed to be able to give her mom and her brother what they most wanted for Christmas, and to be able to buy some sharp clothes for herself. But a side-by-side freezer/refrigerator and a BMX bike weren't cheap. Only fifteen, Melody couldn't qualify for most jobs.

But one day a friend told her about the possibility of selling quality jewelry for Christmas presents. So she stopped by the business, signed for samples, and started selling.

Discovering that she was a talented salesperson, Melody worked hard and sold more than she even dreamed possible. At the senior citizen's high-rise, every other lady needed a gift for a friend, a daughter, or a granddaughter. Nobody could turn down a charming high-school girl who wanted to buy her widowed mother a refrigerator for Christmas. Melody kept good records, delivered the merchandise on time, and produced satisfied customers.

Thankful to God for her success, Melody set aside her tithe, and then had the refrigerator and bike delivered to her home on Christmas Eve day—to the surprise of both her mother and her brother. She had experienced the true joy of sacrificial giving. There was even enough money to purchase a new wardrobe for herself. For the first time since she was a little girl, people seemed to notice her neat clothes. It was a great Christmas!

But on the first day of school in January, Melody's friend, Mary Lou, approached her with some startling information: "Melody," she moaned, "I'm sure you didn't know it, but the jewelry you sold wasn't fourteen-carat gold—it was fake."

"How do you know?" Melody asked.

"We all go to my grandmother's for Christmas," Mary Lou explained. "My mom really liked the necklace I bought from you. But my uncle is studying to be a jeweler, and he checked it over. He said it was just costume jewelry. Then he asked me what I paid for it. Although the price would have been very reasonable for gold, it was three times what the necklace is worth."

Melody was dumbfounded. What should she do?

1. Say nothing since she didn't know that the company had given her false information.
2. Get another jeweler to give her an appraisal, and if the jewelry is fake get the signatures of customers in order to sue the company.
3. Complain to the Better Business Bureau.
4. Offer each customer her money back.

♥ ♥ ♥ THIS WAY OUT ♥ ♥ ♥

☑ Asking God to Meet Legitimate Needs

Dear God, I know you require that I be strictly honest in everything I do and say. But it's hard in such a crooked world—other kids are constantly cheating on tests, shoplifting, and exagger-

ating to make themselves look good. Right now, I'm tempted not to be completely honest about _____ . Give me the strength to act correctly.

▶ Getting the Facts Straight

To understand the following verses, you need to know that in Bible times things like wheat or fruit were weighed out on scales. On one side was a weight as heavy as a pound (just an example, because their system was different)—or a half pound, and so forth. When the amount of wheat reached "one pound," the bar connecting the two sides of the scale would be level. Because they didn't have standard coins, even their money—often pieces of silver or gold—was weighed out on these scales. Unfortunately, it was common practice to use lighter weights on the scale, which cheated customers who were buying. Often a heavier weight was used when the merchant wished to make a purchase.

The Lord abhors dishonest scales, but accurate weights are his delight (Proverbs 11:1).

Honest scales and balances are from the Lord (Proverbs 16:11).

Differing weights and differing measures—the Lord detests them both (Proverbs 20:10).

"It's no good, it's no good!" says the buyer; then off he goes and boasts about his purchase (Proverbs 20:14).

The Lord does not close His eyes even to our "little" dishonesties. He sees when you peek over at Bill's paper just to check if the answer you put down for number five is correct. He notices if you fail to return the extra money the clerk gave you in change. Your exaggeration of the merits of the product you're selling offends God.

On the other hand, God is honored when you honestly admit you've never heard of the singing group. Giving up the perfect chance to cheat and accepting the F on the quiz because you missed the explanation the day the band was out of town is a sacrifice that God accepts. Openly acknowledging that it was your fault, or that you are wrong, honors the Lord who loves justice.

☛ Rethinking the Situation

Melody couldn't think about biology or world history or English. Her mind kept returning to the spiel she'd memorized: "This is the best price you'll find on fourteen-carat-gold jewelry anywhere." Whether she tried to do a geometry problem, dress for gym, or simply close her eyes, her mind pictured the jewelry samples. Were they really fake? Had she unintentionally deceived all those people?

When she got home from school, she went straight to her room. First she cried. Then she tried to pray. And finally she paged through her Bible. Some words jumped out at her: "Be careful to do what is right in the eyes of everybody" (Romans 12:17). She really couldn't get off the hook.

After supper, she told her mother and her brother. They prayed about the problem together. Her mother took her to the a jewelry store downtown. The well-respected gray-haired owner confirmed that it was costume jewelry and told them that the company had just filed for bankruptcy. He said that the products she sold were worth less than half the price charged.

Melody knew that the only honest thing to do would be to go back to each person and offer to return the money she had overcharged. Her mother and brother agreed to sell the refrigerator and bicycle if necessary, and she would take the clothes she hadn't worn yet back to the store.

The next day, Melody found her list and started calling on customers. The ladies who heard her story were impressed. And except for one person, everyone thanked her for her honesty and told her to keep the money. After she'd contacted each one on her list, only three wanted money back. Many told her, "You're the kind of person I like to do business with."

After that, Melody started selling for a very reputable company and was able to buy all her own clothes and to help her mom with expenses. She had thought she'd lose everything by obeying God, but instead it brought her great prosperity.

☛ Putting the Truth Into Practice

MONTHLY HONESTY CHECK-UP

Think back over the last month, and honestly evaluate your behavior:

_____ 1. I haven't cheated on one answer on any test. (+2)

_____ 2. I haven't copied one homework assignment from a friend. (+2)
_____ 3. I copied my report from the encyclopedia instead of writing it in my own words as my teacher directed. (−3)
_____ 4. I wrote a book report without reading the book. (−3)
_____ 5. I haven't taken or indefinitely borrowed anything that wasn't mine. (+2)
_____ 6. I tried to get in to a game or concert or play once without paying. (−3)
_____ 7. I signed my friend's name on the substitute's list so he could skip. (−3)
_____ 8. I made up an alibi so my mother would let me out of the house. (−3)
_____ 9. I told the truth even though I knew I'd be punished for what happened. (+4)
_____ 10. I blamed my brother or sister for something that was really my fault. (−3)
_____ 11. I lied and said I'd finished my homework so I could watch TV (or talk on the phone, or something else). (−3)
_____ 12. I told the truth even though I knew the other kids would hassle me. (+4)
_____ 13. I told the truth even though all my friends lied. (+4)

Did you come up with a perfect score (18), or are there things you need to work on?

If there is dishonesty in your life, confess it as big-time sin. Make the decision to always do what's right, even if it will cost you a lot. Humbly receive the help Jesus wants to give you to live by the truth. When you're willing to obey, He has supernatural resources for you to draw upon.

Where do you need to start? Ask Jesus to help you, and He will.

Self-Examination

Part II: Honest to God and to Others

1. If doing what's right is a pain:
   _____ a. It's because the world's so bad that nobody can do good.
   _____ b. It's because you haven't learned to depend on the dynamite of the Holy Spirit living within you to enable you to live according to God's will.
   _____ c. It's because you're weaker than other Christians.
   _____ d. It's because the peer pressure in your school is worse than in other places.
2. The just shall live by _____ (Romans 1:17).
3. Who is the only One who can really tell what is in your heart?

94

_____ Why is it dangerous to think you're a good judge of your own motives?_____

4. Are you taking the "ostrich approach" to truth about an issue that you need God to clarify for you? _____ If so, what do you plan to do about it?_____

5. What figure of speech does Proverbs use to describe a Christian who has compromised his or her testimony?

_____

6. Are you lowering your standards in some area? _____ How do you think it will affect others? _____

_____

7. The Lord condemns a _____ man (Proverbs 12:2).

8. It's human nature to cover up disobedience by _____ . Why is it wrong?_____

9. Do you have problems obeying orders? _____ What can you do to change your attitude?_____

10. The Lord is displeased by the least little _____

Part III

A Crash Course in Tongue-taming

CHAPTER 16

To Tell the Truth

Talon lived in the inner city, where life was dangerous and survival was top priority. "Keep your nose clean, mind your own business, and remember that you never saw nothing," was the advice his father gave over and over. Tall and powerfully built, Talon found that his dad's formula worked quite well. He especially stayed clear of the Panthers, a dangerous gang involved in drug-dealing.

As a sophomore, Talon met Sam, the best pass receiver on their high-school football team. He was an awesome dude who did what was right and still demanded respect. He invited Talon to church, and there Talon discovered it was possible to have a personal relationship with Jesus Christ. After giving his life to Jesus, Talon sensed God's love and protection. His life now had purpose. The terrible loneliness and desperation disappeared.

But there were new trials, as well. Kids on the street, even little ones, made fun of him when he walked to church carrying his Bible. Jake, the guy across the alley who was a member of the Panthers, now seemed to direct a special hatred toward him, even though Talon had never done anything to cross him. Jake just seemed to possess a special radar system that detected "Jesus freaks," and branded them as enemies.

One Saturday afternoon, Talon was watching college football on T.V. At half time he went to the refrigerator for a Coke, and before returning to the game he paused to look out the third-story window at the spectacular red leaves of the oak tree below. J. D., a slightly retarded man in his twenties, was sitting on the steps across the street staring into space. A lady with a shopping bag full of groceries was approaching. Suddenly Jake popped up from behind a car and grabbed her purse. When she resisted, he shot her in the chest, and ran.

97

Blaring rock music had drowned out the noise and nobody ran to investigate. A woman driving down the street in a red car accelerated as she drove by.

Talon wanted to help, but his father's warning rang in his head: "Remember—you never saw nothing." He called his girlfriend Tanya and told her to call the paramedics, using a pay phone to avoid a police investigation. They arrived on the scene quickly, and Talon felt relieved.

That evening the police knocked at the door. It was a routine check. When they asked Talon if he knew anything about the crime, he said, "No."

He'd lied in similar circumstances before, but this time it really bothered him. Yet he feared that if he told what he knew, the Panthers would kill him. "Lord," he prayed, "please understand. There must be some exceptions to Your rules." But somehow he didn't feel any better.

From then on, the troubled expression on Talon's face concerned his family and friends. When Sam asked him what was wrong, he didn't open up. Months dragged on and the only suspect the authorities found was J. D. Jake told the police that he saw J. D. shoot the lady. Talon doubted that the cops would believe Jake, but they did. A trial was set for February 8th.

Talon realized that his lie, composed of the two-letter word *no*, was about to cost an innocent neighbor his freedom, and maybe even his life! Talon couldn't concentrate on homework or basketball. He was having trouble sleeping. What should he do?

▼ ▼ ▼ THIS WAY OUT ▼ ▼ ▼

☑ Asking God to Meet Legitimate Needs

You need to tell the truth, even when it's unpopular or dangerous to do so. You must trust God to protect you.

Dear God, if I tell the truth when _____ , the other kids will give me a hard time. I'm asking you for the courage to tell what really happened. Please protect me from any retaliation.

☑ Getting the Facts Straight

A truthful witness does not deceive, but a false witness pours out lies (Proverbs 14:5).

A truthful witness saves lives, but a false witness is deceitful (Proverbs 14:25).

A false witness will not go unpunished, and he who pours out lies will not go free (Proverbs 19:5).

A false witness will not go unpunished, and he who pours out lies will perish (Proverbs 19:9).

Like a club or a sword or a sharp arrow is the man who gives false testimony against his neighbor (Proverbs 25:18).

Someone has commented, "Truth is the cement of society." Justice cannot be done unless those who saw what happened are willing to risk something to report it accurately.

The Devil loves to destroy. When people live together peacefully under good government, he becomes furious. The idea that one should never tell on a friend—or a bully—is one of Satan's lies that will erode law and order. You might think that keeping your mouth shut when you see someone steal the test answers, or put a tack on the teacher's chair, or threaten another student, is harmless. It isn't. It's a contribution to another person's misery. It's not fair to the students who studied or to the unsuspecting instructor, or to the fearful classmate. Plus it contributes to a lawless society.

The days are gone when being a truthful witness was easy. Now it requires great courage and sacrifice. But don't forget that you serve a great God who loves to bless those who take great risks for Him.

☑ Rethinking the Situation

On Sunday, Talon went to church as usual. The Pastor spoke about Peter denying Jesus. He said, "We all blame Peter for being a coward.

We forget that his telling the truth meant great physical danger. If the Jewish leaders could find an excuse for executing Jesus, they could certainly do away with His followers. But, in fact, that lie caused Peter a great deal of suffering. He would have been much better off being killed for telling the truth."

The words pierced Talon's heart. He had to tell the truth. He just had to. He asked to talk with the pastor in his study. After relating the whole story, Talon asked his pastor for advice. Later, they drove together to the police station. An officer took down the information and promised that everything would be kept confidential until he appeared on the witness stand in the courtroom. Although Talon imagined a dozen ways in which Jake might knock him off, he felt peace deep down inside.

The pastor told the church that there was an urgent need to pray for the protection of someone in the congregation. At every meeting they prayed. Talon knew that this would continue after the trial had ended.

The day before Talon was to testify in court, a lady came to see the defense lawyer. She had been driving the red car Talon saw the day of the murder. The woman lived in a suburb, but had been driving through the neighborhood at the time. After seeing the lady shot, she said she became so frightened she left the scene of the crime. Reading the story in the paper, she came to the police offering to testify in J. D.'s defense.

After she told her story to the jury and was cross-examined, Talon took the stand. Since the two witnesses agreed perfectly, and both said they'd seen Jake kill the lady, Jake was prosecuted and put behind bars.

Every time after that, when Talon saw J. D. sitting on the front steps, he made a new commitment to tell the truth—regardless of the cost.

☛ Putting the Truth Into Practice

What cases have you faced in which it was difficult to be a truthful witness?_____

_____

_____

In what situations would it be easy for you to lie just a little bit?

_____

_____

What is more important to you—peer pressure or pleasing God?

Put Proverbs 19:5 on a card so you can memorize it: "A false witness will not go unpunished, and he who pours out lies will not go free." Carry the card with you so you can meditate on this verse often, so that its message becomes part of you.

CHAPTER 17

The Last Word

Marissa was petite, pretty, vivacious—also quick-tempered and extremely talkative. Her mind was like an open book, or more accurately, like a constantly playing cassette. If she didn't like something, she said so. Whatever she thought was immediately put into words.

Most of the time, her ready smile, unpretentious manner, and keen sense of humor made her the center of attention and the life of the party. But at times her big mouth got her into trouble.

When Janette told her that she thought Tim was handsome, Marissa, the "walking, talking newspaper," speedily transmitted the headline—"Janette has a crush on Tim"—to the waiting world. Janette was furious, and it almost ruined their friendship.

Then Marissa told Angie that her new dress looked like something out of her grandmother's attic trunk. It caused a few waves, but Angie forgave her, and exchanged her outfit for another.

Marissa was so active, and so busy talking, she rarely noticed how her comments affected others.

When Eric asked her out, she was overjoyed. They went to a Christian concert in the city. Because of the driving time involved, her parents gave her a 1:00 A.M. curfew. Talking, laughing, ordering pizza, and running out of gas, Marissa and Eric returned two hours late. Her worried and upset parents grounded Marissa for two weeks.

"Learning to think ahead and avoid problems is part of successful living," her father counseled. "I know you don't purposely disobey, but dating involves responsibilities—and this is one of them."

Marissa boiled over. This would spoil their plans for next Saturday night. "You just don't understand me," she screamed. "I wish I could trade you for Janette's folks. If I could leave home, I would—*right now!*" Ignoring the tears in her mother's eyes, she stormed up to her room and slammed the door.

Very early the next morning, Marissa's parents received a phone call telling them that her grandmother in Phoenix was ill. Her mother quickly packed so she could leave on the next plane, then woke Marissa to say goodbye.

Never very pleasant in the morning, Marissa just pouted. "You help everybody else, but only wreck all my plans. I guess you're too old to remember what it's like to be a teenager in love." Tears reappeared in her mother's eyes, but Marissa wasn't about to apologize—not yet.

Later, after Marissa had dressed, her father called from the office. "I'll be right home," he said tenderly. "I have something important to tell you."

As she waited for her dad, Marissa absentmindedly switched on the T.V. just as a local newscaster was saying, "Flight 682 has crashed in a field near the Phoenix airport." As a cold shock washed over her, she saw footage of the plane's flaming hulk, and heard the awful words: "All passengers are feared dead."

"*No!*" she screamed. "*It can't be!*"

It was then that her father walked in and put his arms around her. "What if I never get to apologize to Mom?" she sobbed. "The things I said to her were terrible."

Her father didn't seem to hear.

Slowly, the minutes passed. An hour later—which seemed like an agonizing eternity—they got the terrible news: "There are no survivors."

Mercilessly, Marissa's mind replayed her last two conversations with her mother over and over: "I wish I could trade you for Janette's folks," . . . "If I could leave home, I would—*right now!*" . . . "You only wreck all my plans," . . . "You're too old to remember what it's like to be a teenager in love."

If only she could erase the tape! Her habit of always having to have the final word had backfired. Why couldn't her last words to her mother have been, "Mom, I'm sorry, and I love you"?

THIS WAY OUT

Asking God to Meet Legitimate Needs

Although holding everything in can be unwise and harmful, there's a difference between "speaking what's on your mind" and honestly expressing your views in a way that won't hurt others. What you must learn is the art of "speaking the truth in love" (Ephesians 4:15).

Dear God, "Set a guard over my mouth, O Lord; keep watch over the door of my lips" (Psalm 141:3). Help me to think carefully before I speak to make sure that what I say won't leave wounds and scars.

Getting the Facts Straight

Reckless words pierce like a sword, but the tongue of the wise brings healing (Proverbs 12:18).

He who guards his lips guards his life, but he who speaks rashly will come to ruin (Proverbs 13:3).

When words are many, sin is not absent, but he who holds his tongue is wise (Proverbs 10:19).

Do not let any unwholesome talk come out of your mouths, but only what is helpful for building others up according to their needs, that it may benefit those who listen (Ephesians 4:29).

James says: "If anyone is never at fault in what he says, he is a perfect man." It takes little effort to say something that will cause days or years or even a lifetime of pain. And words once spoken can never truly be erased.

Other kinds of sins—like stealing, illicit sex, or getting drunk— require a series of complex actions and the use of many body parts— not just the tongue. For example, when your hand is on the cassette you've decided to steal and your eyes are checking to make sure that no one is watching, your feet could still enable you to run from temptation. On the road to most sins, there are usually several exits along the way. But with the tongue, you can ruin someone's reputation, mar another's self-image, or spread deadly gossip in mere seconds.

Give your tongue to Jesus and make it abide by all *His* rules. Before you speak, ask yourself some questions:

1. Do I need to calm down before I say anything?
2. Will my negative statement be useful in solving this problem or in clarifying an issue, so that I can build a better relationship with the person?
3. Would it be wiser to say nothing at all?
4. Will my comment be constructive?
5. If Jesus were standing by me in person, would I still offer my opinion?

For most of us, controlling our tongue means saying a lot *less.* "When words are many, sin is not absent" is a very sobering fact. Thinking and *praying* before you speak is one of the most helpful habits you can establish.

☑ Rethinking the Situation

For the next few days, Marissa operated in a fog. Her older brother came home from college, friends brought food and consoling words, Dorothy sang at the funeral—and every time Marissa remembered her last words to her mother she cried. That picture of her mom, with tears in her eyes, was forever printed on her memory. If only she'd watched her tongue more carefully! If only she could see her mother one last time so she could apologize. If only . . .

A week later, she and her father were seated at the supper table trying to eat the chicken noodle soup and burned grilled-cheese sandwiches Marissa had prepared. But Marissa was lost in tears. Her father put his arm around her and they both cried.

Finally he spoke. "Marissa, I know you pretty well, and I'm sure you're having trouble with the last things you said to your mother."

"If only I could apologize to her," Marissa agonized.

"Your mother knew Jesus very well, and I can't help but think that He's already told her you're sorry," her dad replied. "But I do feel this experience will help you see how important it is to monitor your mouth. Talking is dangerous business—and you usually do more than your share. Realizing all the suffering a few rash words have caused will remind you to be more careful in the future."

Marissa smiled through her tears. "Thanks, Dad. I know you're right. Mom always hoped that I'd learn to *think* before I speak. If I really work on it, maybe Jesus will tell her about my progress so she can be proud of me."

✒ Putting the Truth Into Practice

TONGUE-TAMING REPORT CARD

Rate the behavior of your tongue. Using the chart on the next page, give yourself an A, B, C, D, or F for each day this week. (If you *avoid* all of these pitfalls, you can get straight A's.)

1. Unnecessary put-downs.
2. Jokes that take advantage of someone.
3. Cutting remarks.
4. Making mincemeat of someone in order to manipulate him or her.
5. Unkind comments.
6. Criticism of authority.
7. Broadcasting the faults of others.

	S	M	T	W	T	F	S
1.							
2.							
3.							
4.							
5.							
6.							
7.							

CHAPTER 18

Some Wisecracks, a Handsome Hunk, and Aunt Nellie

Denika was by nature very funny and sarcastic. She made fun of teachers, mimicked politicians, and impersonated other students. Sometimes she exaggerated and added some things just to make her "act" more hilarious. She always quipped, "If you don't have brains or beauty, you have to be a comedian."

When Christmas vacation rolled around, her best girlfriend Kristi arranged a double-date, pairing up Denika with her boyfriend's cousin who was visiting from Kansas City. Denika was delighted.

Appearing at the church Christmas banquet with a handsome hunk gave her a sense of security and self-esteem. She was very impressed with Marc. Not only was he a football player, he was gentle, full of fun, and polite. He even seemed to like her! While they were waiting for the food to be served, Denika did some of her impersonations, cracked her most popular jokes, and kept everyone entertained. Denika was on cloud nine. She hoped she was making a good impression on Marc.

After the evening's program, they decided they were hungry for a second dessert. At the pie shop, Denika continued the show. She got started on her "Neighbor Nellie Routine": "Nellie dresses like the 1940s," Denika mocked, "and now her clothes are coming back in style again! She loses something three or four times a day, and always comes over to tell my mother about it. One day she said she'd lost her piano—can you believe that?—because she forgot the painters had moved it!"

Kristi and Dan were laughing, but Denika noticed that Marc was not. That stopped her short.

"Is your neighbor's name Nellie Nelson?" Marc asked.

"Why, yes," Denika answered uncertainly. "How did you know?"

"She's my father's aunt," Marc replied. "She suffered a brain aneurysm about twenty years ago, and she's had problems keeping things straight ever since. I realized who you were poking fun at when you said she'd lost her piano—we heard about that. When she was young, before her medical problems, she was a brilliant musician. She has a heart of gold. She's going to help send me through college."

Dead silence fell. Denika would have done anything to disappear, but she was face-to-face with the tragedy her tongue had created.

▼ ▼ ▼ THIS WAY OUT ▼ ▼ ▼

☑ Asking God to Meet Legitimate Needs

Making fun of people or criticizing them is not necessary nor does it help build a better world.

Dear God, keep me from making jokes at the expense of others, or broadcasting their faults.

☑ Getting the Facts Straight

With his mouth the godless destroys his neighbor, but through knowledge the righteous escape (Proverbs 11:9).

A man who lacks judgment derides his neighbor, but a man of understanding holds his tongue (Proverbs 11:12).

Love your neighbor as yourself (Matthew 19:19).

The Bible has some pretty stern things to say about those who use unkind words to hurt another. "If you can't say anything nice, don't say anything at all" is still excellent advice.

If Sandy doesn't know how to dress, it's better *not* to tell the world. When you notice how selfish Bill really is, pray for him and keep it to yourself. If you were the only one present when your youth pastor lost his temper, make sure that no one else ever finds out.

Before you open your mouth, ask yourself if what you're about to say would make for good conversation if Jesus were sitting next to you. If not, forget it. Consider also the effect your words will have on those who listen. Quite a few people have been turned-off by Christians who criticize and put down their neighbors.

☛ Rethinking the Situation

Although Kristi tried to talk about other things, they rode home mostly in silence. They dropped Denika off first, and as she walked up to the door tears filled her eyes.

Her mom was in the dining room wrapping Christmas presents. "Denika, what's the matter?"

Denika told her mom the whole story. "If only I could take back everything I said," she moaned. "If only I'd known that Nellie was Marc's great aunt. He's the neatest guy in the world, and he's coming here for college. But now I've ruined everything."

"Denika," her mom said seriously, "when we repent, God sometimes gives us a second chance. But there's something much more important than Marc at stake here. It's your habit of making jokes at the expense of others. The Bible says that our every comment should build up other people."

Denika began to realize what she'd been doing. In her effort to be humorous, she hadn't really cared who got hurt. This time her words backfired—but she'd probably already hurt a lot of other people.

Denika now felt genuinely sorry for what she'd done. Her sense of humor had not only damaged the reputation of her neighbor—it had brought dishonor to the name of Christ. As she and her mother prayed together, she asked Jesus to forgive her for making fun of people and exaggerating their idiosyncrasies and weaknesses. Determined to say only things that would be helpful, she was willing to give up her center-stage position, to forfeit the laughs and let God mold her sense of humor to fit His specifications.

✔ Putting the Truth Into Practice

SENSE OF HUMOR SURVEY

1. Do you make "just joking" comments that hurt some people, like "Nobody would want Jeff on their team," or "Sally, that's the way to throw your weight around"? List any similar statements of yours that come to mind. _____

   _____

   _____

   _____

2. Do you make fun of others just to get laughs? What kind of things do you say? _____

   _____

   _____

3. Do you tell stories based on the *not-so-smart* comments or actions of others—things they'd rather forget? _____
4. Are you respectful of older people, or do you make them the subjects of your jokes?_____

   Ask God to make the necessary changes in your sense of humor so it, too, can be a testimony for Jesus.

CHAPTER 19

Annihilating Anger

Winona met Zach at a friend's party. A solidly built guy with wavy brown hair, he was full of fun and spontaneity. They were mutually attracted to each other, so Zach started hanging around with Winona and her friends, and even started attending her church.

Although she liked Zach a lot, Winona quickly noticed a rather prominent defect: Zach's temper erupted with alarming frequency. Because everyone in her family was easy going, she didn't quite know how to handle it. Soon the problem was getting out of hand.

A month after they met, they were driving down the interstate, when a guy driving an old clunker accidentally pulled out as Zach changed lanes. Furious, Zach laid on the horn and cut in, almost forcing the other guy into a guardrail. Terrified, Winona screamed.

Zach turned his anger on her: "Shut up!" he exploded. "I know what I'm doing!"

Two weeks later, he invited Winona to have dinner with his family. They spread their books out on the dining room table in order to study for finals until supper was ready. When Zach slipped into the kitchen to ask his mom what she was serving for supper, Winona could hear every word. His mother replied that it was homemade soup, potato salad, and sandwiches.

Zach blew up. "That's not a company dinner!" he said angrily. "I was planning on steak."

Feeling like she ought to do something, Winona entered the kitchen to tell Zach's mom she thought the menu was just fine.

"You stay out of this," Zach ordered. Turning to his mom, he demanded, "I expect you to cook the same for my guests as you do for yours."

"Well, Zach," his mother said, soothingly, "here's some money.

Run over to the meat market. If you buy some steaks right away, I can get them done before your father comes home from work."

Winona was shocked, but said nothing. She declined an invitation to ride along, and tried instead to concentrate on English literature.

That weekend, Winona took her place in the bleachers to watch Zach play baseball. On Zach's first trip to the plate, he was called "out on strikes." His verbal attack on the umpire brought his teammates off the bench to try to calm him down. But brushing them aside, he became even more violent. The umpire not only kicked him out of the game, but suspended him for the season. Winona was mortified. Zach claimed to be a Christian and he showed less self-control than any of the other players!

The umpire, however, was a close friend of Winona's father and she felt it was her duty to bail Zach out. She pleaded for a second chance, and the next week Zach was again playing first base.

By the bottom of the ninth, Zach's team was ahead 5 to 4, and their opponents had bases loaded with one out. The second baseman fielded a grounder, tagged second, and threw wide to Zach. The umpire ruled the player safe at first, claiming that Zach's foot had not touched the bag. Two runs scored—giving the victory to the other team.

Zach was furious—and this time his temper tantrum made the umpire so upset that he banned Zach from the ballpark for the entire season!

By now, Winona was realizing that Zach *always* called the shots, and that their relationship went smoothly only because she never offered any resistance. She decided she should be a little more assertive.

She got her chance three weeks later.

On their way to a Burger King one evening, she asked Zach to stop at a mall so she could buy an anniversary present for her parents. Winona wanted to get water glasses to match her mother's new china. The first shop had nothing, so they went on to one of the finer department stores. They'd barely found the china department when Zach decided he'd had enough. "I'll give you five minutes to decide," he snapped. "Then we're leaving."

Winona felt fire inside. "What makes you think you can tell the whole world what to do?"

Zach hurled insults at her, and Winona became more angry than she'd ever been in her life. She began screaming at the top of her lungs, "Leave! Leave me alone! I can't stand it anymore!"

Catching a glimpse of the gathering crowd, Zach grabbed her and attempted to clap his hand over her mouth. Winona pushed him away and bumped into a stand, knocking a crystal punch bowl to the floor—where it shattered.

When store security rushed to the scene, witnesses insisted that Zach had been verbally abusive and said they thought he was trying to harm Winona. In the end, two policemen took him to the station in a squad car.

▼ ▼ ▼ THIS WAY OUT ▼ ▼ ▼

☞ Asking God to Meet Legitimate Needs

It's necessary to realize that a loving God will give you His very best if you let Him choose for you. Permit Him to look out for you and to arrange the details of your life. Trust Him to handle your problems. You're not the one at the controls, and you can be thankful for that!

> *Dear God, help me to see that "man's anger does not bring about the righteous life that God desires" (James 1:20). Keep me from using my temper in order to get my own way. Show me how to surrender my frustrations to you instead of quietly smoldering or venting my displeasure.*

☞ Getting the Facts Straight

A quick-tempered man does foolish things, and a crafty man is hated (Proverbs 14:17).

A hot-tempered man must pay the penalty; if you rescue him, you will have to do it again (Proverbs 19:19).

Anger is cruel and fury overwhelming (Proverbs 27:4).

Do not make friends with a hot-tempered man, do not associate with one easily angered, or you may learn his ways and get yourself ensnared (Proverbs 22:24–25).

An uncontrolled temper leads to hasty and foolish action, not to mention all the cutting remarks and spiteful words that can never be erased.

The root cause of most anger is an I-will-defend-my-rights-at-all-times-and-in-all-places attitude, or, a nobody's-gonna-push-me-around attitude. It shows up in several forms—tantrums designed to force others to give in, calculated revenge on those who upset your plans, a touchiness if ignored, resentment, and outbursts of wrath against people or things that cause frustration.

Unless you give *all* your rights to Jesus, you'll never conquer anger. If you really believe that God runs the universe and that He *always* does a better job than you could, irritation, impatience, and flying off the handle can be replaced with statements like this: "I didn't get what I wanted, but I know God has something better planned"; "Instead of getting upset about all the nasty rumors he spread about me, I'm reading my Bible to remember all the good things God has to say about me"; "If I have to stand in line for an hour, it's God's time, not mine"; "My parents won't let me go on the ski trip, but I'm trusting God to run my social life." Remember that God has the right to plan your weekend. He has the authority to tell you to turn the other cheek and the power to enable you to obey.

✔ Rethinking the Situation

That night Zach couldn't get to sleep. He'd made a total fool of himself just because he couldn't control his temper. His dad had commented, "If all your religion made you into a better person, I might be impressed." Winona had told the police that she really didn't think Zach meant to hurt her, but he was sure she'd never go out with him again. Zach really didn't know what to do.

Winona wasn't sleeping either. Instead, she was looking up all the Bible verses on anger. She found some perfect descriptions of Zach: "A quick-tempered man does foolish things"; "A hot-tempered man must pay the penalty; if you rescue him, you will have to do it again."

But one verse really fit *her.* "Do not make friends with a hot-tempered man, do not associate with one easily angered, or you may learn his ways and get yourself ensnared."

Wow! she thought. *I guess that's what happened. I thought I shouldn't be going out with Zach. Now I know why.* But she also realized that *her* anger was sin. She'd helped cause the whole commotion. She admitted to God that she was wrong and in the morning she called Zach to ask his forgiveness.

Zach said he was sorry, and admitted that he was all mixed up. She suggested that he see their youth pastor, so he did.

After they had talked for a while and read some scriptures, Zach finally realized what a horrible sin anger was and that he couldn't cop out by saying, "I just have a bad temper, that's all." He saw that the root of his anger was an incredible selfishness and a desire to control every situation. It occurred to him that he needed to let God rule His universe. That meant surrendering all his rights, all his dreams, all his desires, and every moment of every day to God.

Anger had revealed that there was a deeper sin—the false idea that he could do a better job of running things than the Creator of the universe.

☛ Putting the Truth Into Practice

1. What frustrating experiences anger you? (traffic jams, long weekend assignments, a locker that won't open):_____

   _____

   _____

   _____

2. What anger patterns do you find in your life? (e.g.: "My mom complains about my messy room, I give a bunch of excuses, she delivers a sermon, and I blow up." "My little sister borrows my cassettes without asking, and I bawl her out.")_____

   _____

   _____

   _____

3. When have you become angry during the last month?

   _____

   _____

   _____

As you read over each situation, explain how really believing that God is in control and surrendering your rights to Him could have changed your response. (God does expect that our *attitude* be one of giving Him our rights, but that does not exclude practical solutions such as locking up your cassette collection to keep careless younger siblings from taking them.) Write down any ways of avoiding the problem that occur to you, as well._____

_____

_____

_____

_____

CHAPTER 20

Joining the Patience Platoon

Mario was used to Los Angeles—he had fit in there. Nobody noticed a few grammatical errors and a Spanish accent. But when his father found better work in a small town in Colorado, it meant moving in November of his senior year to a place where they were the only Mexican family. Canyon Creek High seemed so small. There were only fifteen students in physics and higher math, and the same teacher taught both courses. The only thing happening was pine trees, snow, and skiing. Mario could learn to ski, but a tightly knit system of cliques excluded him from most social events.

During basketball practices, Mario discovered that Shinji, a Japanese-American guy, wasn't as quiet as he seemed to be in class. Pretty soon they became friends, and being treated as an outsider didn't seem so bad. At least there were two of them. Both loved basketball, which meant Mario had someone to practice with on weekends.

The first game was at home, against Mountainview. Because the teams were arch-rivals, the whole town turned out for the sports event of the season. Barry and Tom were the starting guards. Nervous and trying too hard, they played poorly. Barry drew four fouls and by half time Mountainview led by ten points. Then the coach put Mario and Shinji into the game. Nobody expected Mario's outside jump shots, and he quickly sank two baskets! Shinji intercepted the ball and passed it to their star center—for *two more* big ones.

Back in the game, Canyon Creek battled hard and won a close contest. The local radio station declared Mario and Shinji players of the week, and they did a newspaper interview together that appeared in a feature article. They replaced Barry and Tom as starting guards—and more girls started saying hi to them in the halls.

Still, the other team members treated the two like dirt—in subtle ways that the coach didn't detect. They told mean jokes about people with accents and slanted eyes. Mario and Shinji were never invited when the team went out to eat after a victory. Nasty jokes were circulated about their families. Both boys suspected that Barry was bitter about losing his first-string position, and that he was the brains behind the smear campaign.

One Saturday after their workout at the gym, Barry and Tom were waiting for them. Defiantly, Barry walked up to Shinji. "You're nothing but a Jap," he sneered. "Your grandfather helped attack Pearl Harbor and he killed my grandfather's brother. You have no right to be in my country, or my school, or on my basketball team."

Shinji remained calm. He closed his eyes for a minute and Mario knew he was praying. Then he replied evenly, "You may believe untrue rumors if you wish."

Then Barry cornered Mario. "You dirty wetback! You're not even a U.S. citizen. Go back where you belong. I'll bet your sister works at the truck stop as a prostitute."

That did it! Mario downed Barry with one punch to the jaw, and began swearing at him in Spanish. He was too angry to be aware that the whole scene had been witnessed by half the team, who were hiding behind a nearby stand of evergreens.

When eight guys swore to the coach that Barry had been "sucker punched" for no reason, Mario was branded as a hot-headed Mexican. Worse, he was suspended from the team for three weeks.

◆ ◆ ◆ THIS WAY OUT ◆ ◆ ◆

✔ Asking God to Meet Legitimate Needs

Dear God, I know I must learn to control my temper, and only the greater power of your love can conquer my anger. Fill me with your love, your compassion, and your self-control.

✔ Getting the Facts Straight

A gentle answer turns away wrath, but a harsh word stirs up anger (Proverbs 15:1).

A hot-tempered man stirs up dissension, but a patient man calms a quarrel (Proverbs 15:18).

A fool gives full vent to his anger, but a wise man keeps himself under control (Proverbs 29:11).

Better a patient man than a warrior, a man who controls his temper than one who takes a city (Proverbs 16:32).

Everyone knows that it's super-important to watch your tone of voice and to calm down before you speak. If *you* choose not to fuel a quarrel, it's pretty hard for the other person to keep it going.

But it's impossible to put this good advice into practice without patience, self-control and gentleness. The only endless, overflowing source of these qualities is the Holy Spirit. "But the fruit of the Spirit is love, joy, peace, patience, kindness, goodness, faithfulness, gentleness, and self-control. Against such things there is no law" (Galatians 5:22–23).

Replacing a *negative* emotion with a stronger dose of a *positive* one brings the desired results. Bottling up your anger only produces ulcers, tension headaches, and acid indigestion. But the wonderful thing is that the Holy Spirit has all the self-control, gentleness, and patience you need. Open your heart to the fullness of the Spirit. As you learn to receive more and more from Him, your habits and goals will change. If you again resort to anger, ask God's forgiveness, trust the Holy Spirit for His self-control, and go on in faith.

✔ Rethinking the Situation

Mario began plotting to get even with Barry. After all, it was up to him to defend his sister's reputation. Besides, the whole team went out to celebrate when they found out that Mario wouldn't be playing for a while. That called for revenge!

But on the way home from school he had a long honest talk with Shinji. "I wish I had your kind of personality," Mario confided. "You seem to be able to stand anything. I know that the team is still persecuting you, and now I'm not there to stick up for you."

"Mario," Shinji replied, "please listen. It's not *me*. I used to be just like you. But then I invited Jesus into my life and He started to make a lot of changes. I realized that His supernatural power was available to me. I asked Him for love-your-enemies love, and He gave it to me. I've been praying for Barry and Tom and all the guys on the team since the first day. God has given me a deep compassion for them. It's a miracle, and the Lord gets all the credit."

"I guess just having religious beliefs isn't enough," Mario conceded. "I need a personal relationship with Christ, like you have."

That night Mario invited Jesus into His life. He also prayed, "Give me the love for Barry and the other guys on the team that You have for them."

When Mario woke up the next morning, he felt like a different person. Now he could plug in to God's love and get an unlimited supply. He knew that with his temperament he'd sometimes react without remembering his new secret—but he was determined to let God replace his anger with divine love. Now he too could be a member of the Patience Platoon.

▶ Putting the Truth Into Practice

1. List the people who have usually been the brunt of your anger.

   _____

   _____

2. Record the reasons that you usually lose your temper with them.
   (e.g.: "I yell at my little sister for not being ready on time.")

   _____

   _____

   _____

3. Read the list over again, asking God for love, patience, and gentleness in each of these stressful situations. Then make another copy and use it as a daily guide for prayer. Every morning ask God for the kindness, self-control, and wisdom to avoid these ugly confrontations. Sometimes the situation needs a creative solution from God.

CHAPTER 21

Your Quarrelsome Heart Will Tell on You

Bart was a brain, a straight-A student, a star on the swim team, and a good actor. Yet he didn't have any good friends, and he wondered why.

For quite a while he'd had a crush on Shauna, so he offered her a ride home from the youth meeting. When they neared the freeway ramp, traffic was backed up as far as they could see. Bart laid on the horn and vented his displeasure. Realizing that they wouldn't be moving for a while, he launched into a long speech making fun of practically everyone, starting with the highway department and ending up with the President of the United States!

When Shauna interrupted, advising him to relax and enjoy the wait, he curtly informed her that only people without goals and ambition accepted things as they came. This was more than Shauna could take, and they ended up arguing until the cars involved in an accident ahead were towed away and traffic flowed freely again. Then Bart changed into a charming gentleman, but Shauna had already decided never to ride with him again.

At next Saturday's meeting, Bart didn't even notice that Shauna and Deann were the first to leave. He was discussing politics with Jerry. "A person who would vote for anyone but a Republican is either crazy or an atheist," Bart declared.

"Well, my dad's a Democrat," Jerry steamed. In a moment, the argument became so loud that everyone could hear them. Trying to be a peacemaker, Keith stepped in and affirmed that each person should vote according to his conscience.

"When *hollowheads* do that," Bart scoffed, "they vote Democratic." This made Keith so angry that he joined the combat. Only when Pastor John turned off the lights and announced that he was about to close up did the heated discussion end.

As they were leaving the church, Bart turned to Carolyn. "I thought the Bible quiz was a lot of fun," he remarked. "But I just can't believe anyone would think that Abraham was one of the twelve apostles! What are you, brain-dead or something?"

At this, Carolyn burst into tears. "I may be dumb, but I'm not like you—*I* have lots of friends who care about me."

"Then they must not be very bright either," Bart retorted.

"Bart, you're mean," Jeannie interrupted.

Unable to let a matter rest without having the last word, Bart returned, "Look who's talking! Aren't you the heavyweight who eats three pieces of cake before everyone gets a chance to have one?"

By this time Jeannie was fighting back tears, too.

▼ ▼ ▼ THIS WAY OUT ▼ ▼ ▼

▶ Asking God to Meet Legitimate Needs

It's not necessary to have the last word, or to prove you're the one with the correct information. Learn to give "the right to be right" to God.

Dear God, help me remember that you see my attitude. Keep me from pride, putting others down, and flaunting my opinions. Show me how to be sensitive to those around me and to be less

*concerned about proving my point. Keep me from being quarrel-
some and stirring up dissension.*

☑ Getting the Facts Straight

He who loves a quarrel loves sin; he who builds a high gate
invites destruction (Proverbs 17:19).

An angry man stirs up dissension, and a hot-tempered one
commits many sins (Proverbs 29:22).

For as churning the milk produces butter, and as twisting the
nose produces blood, so stirring up anger produces strife (Proverbs 30:33).

Although you might be more subtle than Bart, you may display
some of the qualities of a quarrelsome heart—thanklessness, sowing
discord, resentment, getting into arguments, reacting strongly to unpleasant situations, or putting others down to show your superiority.

James T. Draper, Jr., in his book *Proverbs: Practical Directions for
Living* says, "Quarrelsomeness is a problem of the heart. It indicates
that the individual is not at peace with God. . . . Quarrels do not
depend on issues, but on people. . . . A man whose heart has a quarrel
within it is easily involved in arguments and strife."[1]

The turmoil deep within the soul of an argumentative person
comes out in many ways: Showing off, forcing your opinion on others,
ridiculing the ideas and actions of your friends, hitting sensitive areas
in the life of another, and dishing out unconstructive criticism. Your
quarrelsome heart will tell on you.

The cure is peace with God—totally trusting His sovereignty. God
is able to defend truth without your getting into ugly verbal battles
about abortion. God can correct His kids without your constant criticism. God knows what He is doing when He allows pain, trauma, or
annoyances to touch your life. If you have no quarrel with God, it's a
lot easier to get along with His creation.

Colossians 3:15 tells us, "Let the peace of Christ rule in your
hearts." Jesus offers tranquility and inward joy. Whether or not you
accept it is up to you. But peace on the part of the earth where you
live depends a great deal on your decision.

---

[1]James T. Draper, Jr., *Proverbs: Directions for Living* (Wheaton, Illinois: Tyndale House
Publishers Inc., 1987), pp. 140, 141.

↳ Rethinking the Situation

"Let's all go out for pizza," suggested Rick. "Only I'm not inviting dagger-tongue. I can't stand to see pretty girls like Carolyn and Jeannie cry."

"Well that counts Bart out," Mary insisted.

"So you're the saint of the group," Bart countered.

At this point Pastor John interrupted, "Bart, why don't you ride with me?"

Pastor John drove to a different restaurant. He told Bart he wanted to help him. Reviewing the events of the evening, he carefully explained why Bart's comments had made everyone upset. Slowly, Bart began to realize his problem of hurting others was the cause of broken friendships—and most of all, it was a sin before God.

"Bart," Pastor John continued, "the root of the whole problem is that deep down inside you're not content. And since God is the One who runs this universe, it's either a quarrel with your Maker, or lack of faith in His judgment. You don't think He can change people's minds without your badgering them and belittling them. You're not sure that He can give you a sense of significance unless you ridicule the ignorance of others. So you spout off."

Bart had never thought of it that way before, and he sat for a while in stunned silence. Slowly, it dawned on him that his quick tongue showed evidence of a tendency to dominate every situation and control every conversation. In a way, he was competing with God.

"First of all, confess it as sin," Pastor John counseled. "Then learn to depend on God's supernatural power to change your heart and control your tongue. God doesn't give commands without supplying His resources to obey them. I'll give you some verses to memorize, internalize, and put into practice. If you blow it, ask God to forgive you and go on in faith, trusting God for more and more victories in your life."

↳ Putting the Truth Into Practice

Read through these root causes of using your tongue as a weapon and check the ones that apply to you:

_____ 1. I'm mad at God for _____ and _____ .

_____ 2. I don't really act as if God is in control when_____
_____ .

_____ 3. _____ is one of God's commandments that I don't agree with.

_____ 4. I want to make people notice me.

_____ 5. I have to make others respect me.

_____ 6. I can't let anyone take advantage of me.

_____ 7. I won't admit I'm wrong so I defend myself to the end.

_____ 8. I must prove my superior intelligence.

_____ 9. I need the compliments I get when I brag about my achievements.

Settle any quarrel you have with God. Stop trying to run the universe your way. Let Him call all the shots and rest in the security that trusting completely in a loving and all-powerful God can bring. Then ask the Lord to give you the sense of significance and acceptance you need, so that you won't have to resort to using your tongue in sinful ways. Place the following verses on cards to memorize, personalize, internalize, and live by. Take them with you for a month or more:

"Let the peace of Christ rule in your hearts, since as members of one body you were called to peace. And be thankful" (Colossians 3:15).

"Woe to him who quarrels with his Maker, to him who is but a potsherd (piece of broken pottery) among the potsherds on the ground. Does the clay say to the potter, What are you making?" (Isaiah 45:9).

"But the fruit of the Spirit is love, joy, peace, patience, kindness, goodness, faithfulness, gentleness and self-control. Against such things there is no law" (Galatians 5:22,23).

"But the wisdom that comes from heaven is first of all pure, then peace-loving, considerate, submissive, full of mercy and good fruit, impartial and sincere. Peacemakers who sow in peace raise a harvest of righteousness" (James 3:17,18).

"A gentle answer turns away wrath, but a harsh word stirs up anger" (Proverbs 15:1).

Daily pray that God will put these things into your life.

CHAPTER 22

Some Down-to-Earth Advice From Outer Space

Carmen had had a crush on Devin for almost a year. He was a clean-cut blonde who was always joking and teasing. He attended her church, which meant she saw him several times a week. Making the most of each opportunity to say hi, she always wore her best clothes and her most pleasing smile.

One Saturday evening, she arrived late for the youth meeting and took the first vacant seat. Two rows in front of her sat Devin—with Michelle! Their laughing and whispering revealed that they enjoyed being together. Carmen doubted that they heard the scripture lesson.

What could Devin possibly see in Michelle? Carmen thought. Why didn't guys seem to like her? She wished she were in Michelle's place—but no, she wasn't jealous! Envy was wrong. She was a Christian and didn't have such feelings.

Carmen wondered what Pastor Dan would come up with this time. Talented and creative, he was able to turn boring, routine youth meetings into exciting events. Attendance had increased rapidly and tonight there were about a hundred kids—but Carmen saw only Devin and Michelle.

"Once upon a time," began Pastor Dan, "on the planet Alpha Sirdraamen IV lived three extra-terrestrials—Ferangin, Kilgonrin, and Ormulin. The atmosphere of Alpha Sirdraamen IV was much different from planet earth. There were actual substances representing human emotions—a beautiful balmy fragrance called love, a green film named envy, a thick, black, foul-smelling smoke known as hate, and a dark blue gas causing allergies, which was resentment.

"The extra-terrestrials had apparatus for gathering these substances: large storage tanks in their hearts that enabled them to accumulate huge quantities of the elements. A tube connected to the mouth facilitated the transmission of the contents of this depository to other beings."

Wow! thought Carmen. *This time Pastor Dan has really flipped his lid.* But she did wonder what was coming next.

"On Alpha Sirdraamen IV," Pastor Dan was explaining, "there were also machines that could clean out heart storage tanks—the extra-terrestrials connected themselves to the device and then pushed buttons that automatically eliminated certain substances. Pressing the black button would remove hate, the green button envy, and so forth. It was also possible to fill up with love, joy, peace, patience, and kindness. However, they needed to stop in *every day*, or risk emergency treatment, which could be very costly and time consuming.

"Ferangin always told people exactly how he felt. He even took a course entitled, 'Throwing Your Weight Around Just Enough to Tip the Scales in Your Favor.' Whenever someone rubbed his fur the wrong way, black smoke poured out of his mouth. If anyone made him feel inferior, he emitted green vapor and blue fog, which caused blurred vision and coughing. The breath of his mouth was indeed formidable— a very useful weapon. But Ferangin was very lonely. He had no friends and the girls avoided him.

"Kilgonrin wanted to be different from his older brother. Whenever hatred, envy, or resentment filled his heart tank, he made sure that none escaped through his mouth. Instead, he always said kind and loving things. As a result, he had a great many friends. The girls stood in line, because besides being so charming, Kilgonrin was extremely handsome. But all the while, he kept stuffing more and more hostility and bitterness into his heart tank. Soon he began to feel pain, and one day his heart tank exploded. He was hospitalized for months and he never regained his health.

"Ormalin, the youngest brother, decided to get his heart tank cleaned out each day. Sure, it took time and discipline to stop every morning and connect himself to the heart-purifying apparatus. But by doing so, he faithfully removed the bitterness, hate, and envy. He also filled up with love, joy, peace, and patience.

"Proverbs 10:18 is an interesting verse and it reads like this: 'He who conceals his hatred has lying lips, and whoever spreads slander is a fool.' At first it sounds like a hopeless case—either you lie to cover your resentment or you reveal your true feelings and become a fool. And I have yet to meet the person who has never been attacked by envy or resentment. When someone unfairly criticizes me, it's easy to dislike the person. When a guest speaker comes, and some kid asks me why I don't preach like he does, I begin to feel envy and resentment.

"This verse in Proverbs is trying to tell us something. You can't deal with hatred, envy, and resentment by letting it all hang out, but you can't bottle it all up inside either. Your only option is to come to Jesus each day confessing any problem in this area, permitting Him to remove the bitterness, and asking Him to replace it with His love."

Carmen thought she should deal with her feelings about Michelle before they got out of control. But the habit of "stuffing" her emotions won out. She convinced herself she wasn't really jealous. After all, Devin would see through Michelle in a couple of weeks and the whole thing would be over. Carmen was "too mature" and "too spiritual" to envy Michelle.

▼ ▼ ▼ THIS WAY OUT ▼ ▼ ▼

☑ Asking God to Meet Legitimate Needs

Don't try to deny feelings of envy, resentment, or dislike for others. It is necessary to recognize these emotions in order to let God deal with them.

Dear God, if I'm really honest right now, I must admit that I'm envious of _____ for _____ . Forgive me and surround me with your security. Then I can just be myself instead of trying to compete with others. I also resent

_____ for _____ . *Clean out my heart and fill it with your love.*

✔ Getting the Facts Straight

He who conceals his hatred has lying lips, and whoever spreads slander is a fool (Proverbs 10:18).

Make a tree good and its fruit will be good, or make a tree bad and its fruit will be bad, for a tree is recognized by its fruit. You brood of vipers, how can you who are evil say anything good? For out of the overflow of the heart the mouth speaks. The good man brings good things out of the good stored up in him, and the evil man brings evil things out of the evil stored up in him. But I tell you that men will have to give account on the day of judgment for every careless word they have spoken (Matthew 12:33-36).

But now you must rid yourselves of all such things as these: anger, rage, malice, slander, and filthy language from your lips. Do not lie to each other, since you have taken off your old self with its practices and have put on the new self, which is being renewed in knowledge in the image of its Creator (Colossians 3:8–9).

Bad-mouthing others and suppressing hostility are the result of storing resentment in your heart. When you let Jesus clean out all the rotten stuff inside, your comments change and you don't have to cork your emotions. Jesus can turn resentment into love, dislike into acceptance, and envy into admiration. When there's nothing bottled up inside, opening your mouth becomes less dangerous. But keeping yourself free of hidden hostility requires several things:
1. Daily permit the Lord to reveal to you what's really inside!
   a. Did someone make a snide remark, falsely accuse you, or make fun of you?
   b. Did another person succeed in an area where you failed?
   c. Did someone ignore you or slight you?
   d. Were you the victim of unfair treatment?
Don't fool yourself by saying, "Oh, I'm so tough it really doesn't bother me. I'm such a strong Christian I'm past feeling resentment." Be honest. Then decide to forgive that person. Ask God for His love for that person. Receive it by faith. If you ignore some small hurt or root of bitterness, it will grow—and become a monster.
2. Ask God for a chance to do something nice for the person who

caused the pain. Luke 6:27–28 is sound advice: "Do good to those who hate you, bless those who curse you, pray for those who mistreat you." When you seriously begin to pray for the person who is causing you trouble, you won't be able to hate them.

3. Ask God to fill your heart with love and forgiveness. You can pray with expectation because you know that it's a request in line with God's will.

✔ Rethinking the Situation

Devin and Michelle had been going together for over four months, and they seemed more infatuated with each other than ever. Carmen found herself avoiding Michelle and cutting her down in conversations with her friends.

One Sunday morning Carmen spotted a gold heart-shaped locket under the pew in front of her. She picked it up and absent-mindedly opened it. Inside was a picture of Devin. So that was what he'd given Michelle for Valentine's Day! She stuck it in her purse, and was too upset to hear anything her minister said. After a miserable Sunday dinner with her family, she went for a walk in the park. Finally, in anger and desperation, she threw the expensive locket in a garbage can. Devin hated carelessness. Maybe now he'd break up with Michelle.

But instead, he put an announcement on the church bulletin board about the loss, and asked everyone in the youth group to help look for it. Carmen felt so guilty she knew she'd have to confess. When she realized what her growing jealousy was doing to her she became frightened, and faced her sin squarely before God.

She told Pastor Dan, and he helped her tell Devin and Michelle. Following Pastor Dan's advice, she promised to give Devin enough money to buy another locket. Pastor Dan asked them not to tell anyone what had happened, and both Devin and Michelle kept the secret. Carmen was humbled. She'd been so self-righteous and had looked down on Michelle as an "immature new Christian," but she was showing more love and restraint than Carmen thought possible.

The experience caused Carmen to make an important decision. She decided never to try to sweep jealousy or resentment under the rug again. From now on, she'd admit she carried wrong feelings and confess them as sin. She'd let God clean out her heart and ask Him to replace aggressive attitudes with His love.

✔️ Putting the Truth Into Practice

1. Identify feelings of jealousy, resentment and hatred. Write them down. (Examples: I'm jealous of my little sister for her good looks"; "I resent the fact that Mrs. Taylor picks on me in gym class."___

   _____

   _____

   _____

2. Ask God for forgiveness and cleansing.
3. Receive love, joy, and peace from the Lord.
4. Pray every day for those who are a problem to you.
5. Ask God for opportunities to go out of your way to do nice things for them.

CHAPTER 23

The High Cost of Listening to Lying Lips

Sara considered herself a Christian—she showed up at church, she served on youth league committees, and she was a "good girl." She didn't see anything wrong, however, with a few "white" lies now and then.

Asking her little sister to say she wasn't home if she didn't want to receive a phone call, writing her own excuse for school when she wanted a day off, and inventing a few dates with neat guys to brag about to her friends at school—none of these practices bothered her. She gave book reports without reading the books, and made up some interesting interviews for her social studies project. Since these things were acceptable in her family, she thought everyone lived the same way.

Sara had always felt rather insecure. Her family wasn't very close and she'd never found it easy to make friends. Although they lacked in social graces and the ability to relate well with people, everyone in her family excelled in efficiency and hard work. Because of that fact, Sara landed one of the few summer jobs in her small town. Waitressing in the cafe on the highway for a very demanding boss wasn't easy, but Sara did a good job and tourists usually left generous tips.

One evening about eight-thirty, she served supper to a big burly guy who looked to be about twenty-five years old. He was very pleasant and extremely complimentary.

Then he introduced himself. "I'm Cory," he said, smiling. "What's your name?" When he suggested that he wait until she got off work and take her to the city twenty miles away for dessert, she accepted.

As they rode along, he told her that he was a salesman for a pharmaceutical company and that the year before he'd won a top-salesman award. He explained that the work was demanding, but that the pay was good. He also told Sara that she was very pretty and that the life of a salesman was lonely.

Even though Cory insisted he had a big sales territory, he kept showing up at the cafe frequently. He and Sara began dating. Sometimes he'd ask Sara to do phoning for him. She'd leave delivery messages—usually to answering machines. One night Sara's friend, Stacy, and her older sister Sharon, who was in nurses' training, stopped in the cafe just before closing time. She proudly introduced them to Cory. Sharon asked him which company he worked for and he stammered a little before answering. Sharon prodded with a few other inquiries. Cory seemed uncomfortable, excused himself and headed for the men's room.

"That guy can't be a pharmaceutical salesman," declared Sharon. "He knows nothing about medications."

After Stacy and Sharon left, Cory returned with a big smile and a promise to take Sara shopping in the morning. "I want you to buy any dress you want," he said playfully. "And I don't care if it's the most expensive in the whole store!"

Sara loved beautiful clothes and had always had to live within a strict budget. Her excitement caused her to forget everything Sharon had said.

After church on Sunday morning, however, Stacy took her aside.

"Sara," she warned, "I don't like the looks of your boyfriend. Sharon says he's a con man. You'd better be careful. He's certainly not a Christian. The sooner you break up with him the better."

"You're just jealous," Sara retorted. Then she added a little lie—"Besides, he goes to church."

Sara's parents also were suspicious of Cory, but she turned a deaf ear. Because they were seldom home, she was free to do as she pleased.

Six months later, Cory was talking marriage. By this time they were even spending nights together when Sara's parents were away. Since they were going to get married anyway, Sara told herself it was okay. Cory gave her a fur coat for Christmas, and she dreamed of the fine home they'd have.

A week later T.V. news announced that East Coast drug dealer Robert Mackay, who was now operating in Colorado, had been arrested in Denver—and the guy they showed on T.V. was Cory!

THIS WAY OUT

✔ Asking God to Meet Legitimate Needs

Being able to discern the difference between truth and falsehood is a necessity if you're to live successfully.

Dear God, help me to live so honestly that I can easily spot lies. Give me the ability to differentiate between the true and the false, the good and the bad.

✔ Getting the Facts Straight

Keep falsehood and lies far from me (Proverbs 30:8).

A wicked man listens to evil lips; a liar pays attention to a malicious tongue (Proverbs 17:4).

If a ruler listens to lies, all his officials become wicked (Proverbs 29:12).

A false witness will perish, and whoever listens to him will be destroyed forever (Proverbs 21:28).

The Bible not only condemns lying, but warns against even listening to lies. We are to pray: "Keep falsehood and lies far from me," and to live in such a way that this prayer can be answered. Several attitudes will help you:

1. If you always speak the truth, you'll be able to detect when another

person is lying. It's common knowledge that con artists have more success with dishonest people. David understood this principle when we wrote, "May integrity and uprightness protect me, because my hope is in you" (Psalms 25:21).

2. If you're willing to face truth instead of escaping into fantasies and daydreams, liars will find you a tough customer. But often the flatterer says exactly what the person wants to hear. Unless you're on the lookout, it's easier to accept the lies and the outrageous compliments than to insist on pure fact. Decide that you want truth even when it's unpleasant.

3. If you're willing to investigate and seek out the truth, you won't accept just any story. Sometimes greed, convenience, or laziness would rather believe falsehood than go to all the trouble of checking things out.

▶ Rethinking the Situation

That night there was a knock at the door. It was the police. They took Sara in for questioning. Although she was released to the custody of her parents, she was subpoenaed to testify in the court trial, and she was afraid that the police didn't believe her when she said she thought the phone calls she'd made were concerning the delivery of medicines to doctors and hospitals. During her ordeal at the police station, she also found out that Robert Mackay was a married man with three children!

Disillusioned, ashamed, angry, and fearful, she thought there was no way to sort out her tangled emotions. How could she have ever gotten into such a horrible situation? In her small town, everybody would find out every detail of the story—and talk about nothing else for days. Sara couldn't just evaporate. Somehow, she'd have to face the music.

As she tossed and turned all night long, Sara realized that she'd never surrendered her life to God—she'd reserved the right to control a whole lot. She decided to put Jesus in command of the whole mess. She repented of her lies, her unwillingness to listen to others enough to check out the facts, and the love for *things*, which made her refuse to open her eyes. She asked God to forgive her for having sex before marriage.

The next weeks were extremely difficult, but she formed a relationship with God that was closer and more precious than any human bond could ever be. Like a starved child, she eagerly read the comforting words of the Bible. Because people constantly asked her leading questions, she prayed fervently for wisdom. Daily, she placed her future in the hands of Jesus. Nothing else was left and He became everything to her.

🖎 Putting the Truth Into Practice

Taking this test may give you some pointers that will help you to avoid listening to lies:
(Circle wrong responses.)

1. Instead of listening to the salesman's pitch and swallowing it hook, line, and sinker, you should:
   a. Compare prices and values.
   b. Call him a liar.
   c. Talk to someone who has bought the product.
   d. Pray before making a decision.
2. Instead of eating up exaggerated compliments, you should:
   a. Hog the conversation.
   b. Politely find out if the person wants something from you.
   c. Give the insecure person the impression that you don't need flattery to continue the friendship.
   d. Nicely point out that a certain statement is false.
3. Instead of accepting preposterous excuses, you should:
   a. Tell the person that you'd rather he/she be completely honest.
   b. Stop speaking to him/her.
   c. Laugh in his/her face.
   d. Stick by your guns if you can see that giving in will encourage more outlandish pretexts.
4. Instead of acting impressed by a line that's obviously false, you should:
   a. Try to change the subject.
   b. Kindly ask a question, which may lead the person who is talking to suspect that you don't believe the story.
   c. Walk away in anger.
   d. Assure the person that you accept him/her as is, and that your friends don't have to be celebrities.

List the occasions when you listen to things that aren't strictly true:
_____
_____
_____
_____

138

Prayerfully seek strategies to help you to avoid listening to lies. Write down any specific things that occur to you.―――――――

―――――――――――――――――――――――――――――――

―――――――――――――――――――――――――――――――

CHAPTER 24

The Catastrophic Compliment

When she was a child, Raquel learned she could attract people to herself by pouring on the compliments. She developed a vocabulary of over-sized adjectives, and was always telling her friends that a new sweater or dress was "gorgeous," "awesome," or "perfectly darling." She was the first to congratulate a guy for making a free throw, answering a question correctly in class, or putting a new bumper sticker on his car. Anyone who liked to hear, "You're fabulous," or "Your report was fascinating," or "Your new haircut is a knockout" could count on Raquel.

When Justin transferred into her chemistry class, Raquel greeted him warmly, assuring him that such a handsome and charming addition to the class was indeed welcome. Shy and insecure, Justin was delighted to hear these words. He made it a point to talk to Raquel because she always had something flattering to say. As he shared with her his dream of becoming a great country-western singer, she told him she knew he'd succeed. Informing him of the student talent assembly, Raquel encouraged him to sign up. Justin finally got up the nerve to submit his name. Scrambling to get enough acts signed up so their advisor wouldn't cancel the assembly, the committee asked no questions and required no tryout.

What Raquel didn't know was that Justin lived mostly in a dream world. He talked big, but had no sense of reality. And when he appeared in the talent show, he sang off-key while picking away on an untuned guitar and making a complete fool of himself. The kids booed him off the stage.

Although Raquel felt sorry for him, she never connected herself with the fiasco. She was totally unprepared for Justin's angry accusations on Monday. He claimed it was all her fault because she talked him into it.

A few minutes later Wendy walked by, wearing an old, bulky ski sweater. "Your sweater is completely stunning," Raquel cooed automatically. "No it isn't," snapped Wendy. "My mom lost the house key, so we stayed with my aunt overnight, and the only thing I had to put on was this sweater—which my aunt wore when *she* was in high school. Raquel, I wish you'd stop your never-ending compliments and for once in your life tell the truth."

▼ ▼ ▼ **THIS WAY OUT** ▼ ▼ ▼

☑ **Asking God to Meet Legitimate Needs**

Dear God, show me how to encourage people and compliment them without stretching the truth in any way. Keep me from using flattery as a means of getting what I want. Help me to build others up by being completely honest.

☑ **Getting the Facts Straight**

He who rebukes a man will in the end gain more favor than he who has a flattering tongue (Proverbs 28:23).

Whoever flatters his neighbor is spreading a net for his feet (Proverbs 29:5).

Wounds from a friend can be trusted, but an enemy multiplies kisses (Proverbs 27:6).

Instead, speaking the truth in love, we will in all things grow up into him who is the Head, that is, Christ (Ephesians 4:15).

The dictionary defines flattery as "exaggerated compliment" and "excessive, untrue, or insincere praise." It's one way you can sin with your tongue. Those who are insecure sometimes use flattery as a way of getting people to like them. All of us are probably guilty of charming others into doing special favors for us. There are times when a favorable comment seems like the only socially correct option—yet truth is more important. It's better *not* to notice your friend's provocative, skin-tight, designer jeans. If the soup your hostess serves is terrible, you can talk about other things.

Flattery is not only dishonest, it can be harmful. Complimenting your friend on the things he keeps going into debt to buy will only encourage his irresponsible behavior. Kindly pointing out that he'd be happier if he obeyed God by paying his bills would serve him much better. Lavish and constant praise can even strain relationships. A friend should be one who will give you a completely honest opinion. A person who likes everything, goes along with anything, and condemns nothing is frustrating, to say the least.

On the other hand, most people aren't very good at accepting even constructive criticism, so it's hard to give it. The above scriptures give two pieces of advice: (1) Truth must always be spoken in love; (2) In the long run, honesty, mixed with kindness, will do more to promote a friendship than flattery.

Rethinking the Situation

Raquel had always considered herself a "ray of sunshine," the person who had a good word for everyone. How could Justin and Wendy be so angry with her?

Finally, she decided to talk things over with her friend, Loretta. Raquel told Loretta everything. "I thought Christians were supposed to encourage everyone," she concluded drearily. "Why do I get so much flack?"

"It's because anytime you say something that isn't strictly true, you're sinning," Loretta offered. "Exaggeration is lying. Facts are necessary before you offer advice or encouragement. If someone tells me only half the story, I might encourage her to keep doing exactly what she's doing, when what she really needs to do is repent.

"Raquel, I think giving compliments is such a habit with you that you never stop to think if what you're saying is totally true. I've never heard you express a negative opinion about anything. You *always* agree with me, no matter what I say. I've been tempted to tell you I'm planning to elope with a circus clown, just to see if I could get you to try to talk me out of it!"

Raquel finally saw the point. She asked forgiveness for all the lies she'd told in the form of "compliments."

As she thought about it later, she knew the only way she could break the habit was to keep very quiet for a very long time. And for her that was a big sacrifice! But she was willing to do it because she loved Jesus and wanted to please Him.

Putting the Truth Into Practice

FLATTERY PROFILE
1. Write down every exaggerated or untrue compliment you remember making in these categories:
   a. haircuts _____
   b. new clothing _____
   c. cars, stereos, other possessions _____
   d. talent displayed (such as singing, a trumpet solo, etc.) _____
   _____
   e. food (someone's cooking) _____
   f. his or her "new flame" _____
   g. schoolwork _____
   h. other _____
2. When have you used flattery?:
   a. to get your own way _____
   b. to keep from getting punished _____
   c. to get out of work _____
   d. to sell something _____
   e. to get your friend to do your homework _____
   f. other _____

Ask God to forgive you for using flattery, and determine to change.

If you're basically free from flattery, and pride yourself on telling the truth, do you do it in love? If you've administered the truth in the form of a tongue-lashing, you also need God's forgiveness. Do you use truth to build up or to tear down? If you have any demolition projects on your record, you must apologize to the person you've wronged—and to God.

CHAPTER 25

Don't Throw Rocks; Throw Roses

When Jason entered Robert E. Lee High School, he naturally gravitated toward the "cool crowd." He had all the prerequisites: athletic ability, fantastic sense of humor, sharp dresser, and lots of charm. He liked being considered one of the popular kids, but hanging around with them meant hearing constant comments that offended his Christian conscience. These kids made fun of everything.

He spent a couple of days trying to make other friends, but the security of being part of a group, knowing whom to sit with at lunch, and the prestige of being looked up to by the student body were more than he could resist. And after a while the sarcastic remarks seemed less offensive—and so did their "plot" to take control in the classroom.

The game plan was to use passive resistance and mockery to upset anything the teachers attempted. One day Mr. Jensen asked, "Who'd be willing to enter the American Legion Oratorical Contest for a lot of extra credit and an automatic A if you win?" When Brianna Baker raised her hand, the group all made noises that signalled *you're a nerd who's about to commit social suicide.* She instantly changed her mind about entering the competition.

They ruined an awards assembly by using the same tactics. The whole student body followed their lead, so that the assembly was terminated and the kids celebrated their victory.

Everyone thought it was great sport to make fun of everything— Kareen's new hairdo, the way Mrs. Butler walked down the hall, Anita's singing, the American flag, the Bible, and even God. The person who came up with the best put-down was admired by all. Nothing was sacred. Nothing was off limits. Jason had a real flair for sarcastic humor and he rose to stardom.

Although he felt uncomfortable when the kids mocked God and

religion, he remained silent. He didn't think it was quite fair to use "Motley Mona" as a target, but he said nothing. Because he tried hard and was really a nice guy, their principal didn't deserve all the insulting nicknames kids heaped on him. But Jason didn't dare risk his popularity by simply referring to him as Mr. Kelly.

And then Jason's parents started getting on his case, because his new speech habits kept surfacing at home. When his father heard him make fun of his little sister, he was grounded for a week. Because his mom was listening when he referred to the principal as "His Idiocy" while talking on the phone, he had to take out the garbage for a month. Even his best friend at church noticed how sarcastic he'd become.

When Mrs. Cary left on maternity leave, Miss Snow, who was straight out of college, took her place in Jason's English Lit class. She started out trying to be diplomatic and to please everyone. She divided the class into four teams, promising pizza to the group that accumulated the most academic points by participating in class discussion and scoring high on tests. Instead, the groups goofed off and vied for the lowest number of points. Not ready to give up, Miss Snow decided that each group should put on a drama to be videotaped. She promised that the best one would be shown at the next P.T.A. meeting. Again the class sabotaged her plans.

Because she had a very pale complexion, the students started calling her Snow White. And since she was overweight, she also got the nickname Frosty the Snow Woman. Unable to control the class, she was soon at her wits' end. One day she was called to the principal's office, and left the class supposedly in discussion groups. But the moment she left, Randy took over. He drew a snowman and snow-woman on the board. Then he led everyone in a "Simon Says" type game: "Frosty the Snow Man says *stand up*." Everyone stood. But if Frosty the Snow Woman gave a command, everyone did the opposite. When Miss Snow returned a few minutes before the class was to end, she was too shocked to respond. They continued the game until the bell rang.

Next Jason went to his biology class. Because he'd forgotten his assignment, the teacher gave him permission to go to his locker so that he could turn it in on time. As he passed Miss Snow's room, he saw her slumped over her desk with her head in her hands, sobbing her heart out.

THIS WAY OUT

🏴 Asking God to Meet Legitimate Needs

Dear God, you know that being negative and mocking everyone is the in thing to do. I don't want to talk like that, but it's so hard always being a fifth wheel. Help me to find some good Christian friends, and give me the courage to be different. I want to obey you, and I'll do it even if everyone else thinks I'm weird.

🏴 Getting the Facts Straight

Whoever corrects a mocker invites insult; whoever rebukes a wicked man incurs abuse (Proverbs 9:7).

If you are wise, your wisdom will reward you; if you are a mocker, you alone will suffer (Proverbs 9:12).

A wise son heeds his father's instruction, but a mocker does not listen to rebuke (Proverbs 13:1).

A mocker resents correction; he will not consult the wise (Proverbs 15:12).

When a mocker is punished, the simple gain wisdom; when a wise man is instructed, he gets knowledge (Proverbs 21:11).

Drive out the mocker, and out goes strife; quarrels and insults are ended (Proverbs 22:10).

The schemes of folly are sin, and men detest a mocker (Proverbs 24:9).

Making fun of kids who are less than sharp, mocking teachers, putting people down, and reacting to everything negatively are so prevalent in public schools that many Christian students accept it as normal. And they often talk just like everyone else. It's very important that you see the serious danger in these attitudes.

First, it hurts a lot of innocent people. Second, "men detest a mocker." It might seem cool in a group situation, but mockers don't form lasting two-way friendships.

Part of the mentality of constantly making fun of everything includes taking nothing seriously, and talking all the time. Listening to another person seems like a rude interruption to today's "Ridicule Report." Constantly jeering and taunting, the mocker sees everything in the light of sarcastic humor. Reality ceases to exist. He or she takes nothing seriously—especially warnings and instructions from parents and teachers.

Because others don't appreciate having their advice scorned, they're determined to tell the mocker a thing or two. Their attempts are met by more ridicule, and a "war of words" is the result. But there's a big price to pay for refusing to listen—"If you are a mocker you alone will suffer."

✒️ Rethinking the Situation

Throughout the day, the sight of Miss Snow crying at her desk stayed in Jason's mind. When he got home from baseball practice, his parents and his pastor were waiting for him. His father began gravely, "Pastor Marshall tells us that you're leading the young people in making fun of everything he tries to do with the youth, and it's destroying the group. We have to admit that because of a lot of things *we've* heard you say, we know you're capable of such a thing."

Pastor Marshall cut in, "There's a very fine line between ridiculing the things we do at church, and making fun of God himself. I'm worried about you, Jason, and all the rest of the young people. You are in a very dangerous position spiritually. The Bible says, 'Do not be deceived: God cannot be mocked. A man reaps what he sows' " (Galatians 6:7).

Jason had tears in his eyes when he told them what he and the class had done to Miss Snow, and how he had seen her with her head in her arms, sobbing. He explained how badly he'd wanted to be accepted, and how he'd become part of "the group." Jason was ready to repent, and he asked his parents and pastor to pray for him. The four of them talked to God, and Jason asked for forgiveness and the strength to be different.

The next morning he went in before class began to apologize to Miss Snow. He was the only one in English class who obeyed her. Everybody else gave her trouble, but Jason stood firm. At lunch time, he ate with kids he hardly knew.

When his friends asked for an explanation, he told them straight out. After a while they let him alone, and in time he found that he really did fit in with a much smaller group of kids who respected him for his Christian stand.

✔ Putting the Truth Into Practice

"Bad company corrupts good character" (1 Corinthians: 15:33).

Any friend of yours who can't come up with straight T's on the exam below should no longer be your friend—even if it's hard for you to part company. Pray and ask God for better friends. If you can't pass the exam yourself, REPENT!
(Circle your answer.)

T F _____ (name of friend) will not ridicule out-of-it kids just to get a laugh.

T F _____ doesn't constantly make fun of authority.

T F _____ does not lead others in class revolutions or in giving the teacher a hard time.

T F _____ does not continually make fun of his/her parents.

T F _____ never scoffs at spiritual things.

T F _____ shows respect for government leaders.

CHAPTER 26

"Acing" the Courses at Big-Mouth Obedience School

Lauren's life wasn't at all easy. Her father had been a fighter pilot in a recent war, and had been shot down and held as a P.O.W. for several weeks. When he was released and arrived home unharmed, Lauren and her mom and brother Don were elated. It seemed that all her prayers had been answered. At first, her dad's unbelievable escapades and many close calls were more exciting than an adventure novel. Although her parents weren't Christians, they went to church with her the next Sunday, and thanked all the people for their loving concern.

After a short time, though, it became obvious that the torture, the brainwashing, and the other traumas of captivity had seriously affected her father. He became depressed, withdrawn, and unable to concentrate. At times, he would seem like himself again, but then he'd lapse into a deeper shell than before. Driven by unreal fears, he'd sometimes become angry and unreasonable. Lauren even had to change piano teachers because her father was sure that Mr. Travis was planning to harm her in some way.

Lauren began to have a lot of angry questions. Why did God allow her father to be shot down? Why didn't God just heal him instantly? Why didn't all these problems draw her parents closer to God? She had a lot of anxiety. Her mom wasn't coping very well, and her little brother was full of resentment. Lauren was strong, like her dad used to be, so she just kept going. But life had lost its luster.

During her junior year, she and Janelle became best friends. Janelle was kind, level-headed, empathetic, well-versed in Scripture, and wise. She had also lost her mother several years before in a car accident. So Lauren sensed that Janelle really knew what she was talking about.

One day Lauren unloaded all her doubts and fears about her family to Janelle. She seemed to understand. "I've often wondered," Janelle reflected, "why God didn't make Christians out of some kind of 'angelic atoms,' so we'd be resistant to emotional and physical pain. But He didn't, and He even sent His Son to earth in a body and with emotions just like ours. I think He wants to teach us to trust Him even when we don't understand, and to help us to remember that this world isn't our permanent home.

"And there's another important thing," Janelle went on. "Somehow when non-Christians see our faith, *in spite of* horrendous problems, it makes them interested in knowing Jesus. God didn't give Paul smooth sailing, but he promised, 'My grace is sufficient for you, for my strength is made perfect in weakness' " (2 Corinthians 12:9).

After that, when things got tough, Lauren repeated the words, "God's strength is made perfect in my times of weakness." Slowly, she learned to draw on God's overcoming power.

Janelle was a faithful friend and a constant source of encouragement. She was quick to spot Lauren's good points and to comment favorably on the things she did well. Although she was honest and didn't fall into flattery, she gave Lauren compliments when she most needed them. Janelle had such a thankful, positive attitude, she was a joy to be around. Her words were like jewels that kept increasing in value and Lauren treasured them.

Lauren had a lot of musical talent, so Janelle encouraged her to enter a solo in the state competition. They prayed about it together, and Lauren decided to sing a song that had a Christian message. She practiced a lot and got through districts with an A-rating.

Two nights before state finals Lauren's father became much worse. He got into his head that Don's boy scout leader was turning his son against him. When Don came home with a Walkman given to him by his scout leader, his father began yelling, "You're never going to another boy scout meeting. Do you understand?"

"You're crazy—and you can't tell me what to do!" Don yelled back.

His father grabbed him and tried to spank him. When Don resisted, he grabbed him around the neck. Lauren let out a scream that brought the neighbors running. The men from next door restrained her father, and a neighbor lady called the cops. Lauren's mom and the police arrived at the same time.

After they had taken Lauren's dad to the psychiatric ward and the neighbors left, her mother became nearly hysterical. Don was so angry she couldn't talk to him. Finally Lauren closed her bedroom door behind her, lay down on her bed and cried and cried. In between sobs she told God, "I can't sing that solo. Nothing will ever work out again. I might as well give up."

▼ ▼ ▼ THIS WAY OUT ▼ ▼ ▼

☑ Asking God to Meet Legitimate Needs

Dear God, my tongue gives me terrible problems. I've just realized how much harm and how much good it can do. And Lord, I not only want to control my tongue, I want to speak in such a way that I help and encourage others. Help me to stop talking long enough to really listen to You. Teach me what to say. Show me how to make my words a blessing. With Your help I can!

☑ Getting the Facts Straight

An anxious heart weighs a man down, but a kind word cheers him up (Proverbs 12:25).

A word aptly spoken is like apples of gold in settings of silver (Proverbs 25:11).

A man finds joy in giving an apt reply—and how good is a timely word (Proverbs 15:23).

The tongue of the wise brings healing (Proverbs 12:18).

The Sovereign Lord has given me an instructed tongue, to know the word that sustains the weary. He wakens me morning by morning, wakens my ear to listen like one being taught (Isaiah 50:4).

You posses something that gives you the power to encourage hundreds of people. It's something that can give new strength to the tired, extra determination to the weak, confidence to the discouraged, and joy to the brokenhearted. Your tongue, operating in total submission to the Holy Spirit, can do all these things.

Your tongue can destroy or build. It can wound or heal, criticize or instruct, put down or encourage. Deciding not to sin with your tongue isn't enough. Determine to let God teach you to speak His words of comfort and peace.

The best way to teach your tongue to say good things is to spend so much time with Jesus that you become like Him. Matthew 12:34 teaches us, "For out of the overflow of the heart the mouth speaks." If your heart is so in tune with Jesus that there is no bitterness, anger, pride, or insecurity to spill out in the form of cutting remarks, put-downs, or lies, your tongue will become an asset instead of a liability. As you saturate yourself with God's Word and listen to the Holy Spirit, your tongue will learn exactly what to say. The discipline of maintaining a strong daily devotional life is like attending an obedience school for big mouths!

☞ Rethinking the Situation

The minute Lauren answered the doorbell the next morning, Janelle sensed that something was wrong. As they walked to school, Lauren related what had happened the night before. Janelle stopped right there on the sidewalk and embraced her.

"Jesus understands your pain," she affirmed. "The Bible says He was 'a man of sorrows and familiar with suffering' (Isaiah 53:3). He loves you. You can be sure that even in this terrible situation He has a purpose, because His Word tells us, 'We know that in all things God works for the good of those who love him' (Romans 8:28). It's not easy, because there's no way that we can understand everything and see things from God's perspective."

Janelle's words brought comfort and soothing to Lauren's rankled emotions. But she was still worried about her solo. "I just *can't* sing in the state competition," she insisted. "I'd rather quit while I'm ahead."

"Don't say you *can't*," Janelle encouraged, "because God says you *can*. The truth that the apostle Paul lived by should be your motto: 'I can do everything through him who gives me strength' (Philippians 4:13). I'll pray for you, and during the contest I'll get some other kids to pray with me."

Janelle explained things to the choir teacher and stayed with Lauren during her rehearsal. She called her mom from school and her parents invited Lauren's family for supper. Janelle accompanied Lauren to the hospital to visit her father. She handled the conversation very wisely, and even got Lauren's dad to let her read from the Bible.

Encouraged, Lauren decided to sing her solo for Jesus, and to rely on Him whatever the outcome. As she rode to the city where the competition was to be held, she remembered many of the helpful things Janelle had said. Over and over she repeated, "I can do everything—even sing well today—through Him who gives me the strength."

Lauren did get her A-rating in the state finals, and she was thrilled. But on the way home she decided that, even more than having a career in music, it was important to have a tongue like Janelle's.

☑ Putting the Truth Into Practice

1. List all the good things your tongue could do. (Such as cheer up an elderly shut-in; build self-esteem in your brother or sister; explain the way of salvation to your classmates; admit when you're wrong and ask forgiveness; tell your teacher you enjoyed her lecture; compliment your mom on her cooking.)

   _____

   _____

   _____

   _____

2. Admit and deal with anything in the reservoir of your thoughts that you wouldn't want to come out when you turn on the faucet and the words flow out.
3. Ask God to guard your mouth and guide your lips. Pray constantly for opportunities for your tongue to be a real blessing to those around you.

Self—Examination

Part III: A Crash Course in Tongue-Taming

```
A G O M O N S T E R J I H M K L H S
F K N J Q P R Z J O Z H G I J Q E R
D N B A D B S W S Y B L F F A E A D
V P C U T U Y R R D E E C K N L R B
D E W S I N X A W T K C R I G H T S
B O A C Q P B T L I E S V X E Z A U
L P O M O U T H P A S W Q Y R M N F
W L N V L N U M P J T E I I F G H F
I E Z Y Z I L K F P O S T E D C T E
M W X S Y S P B Q O R D E T E S T R
G L X P E H R S T J O R S R L H W A
T O N G U E Q W U V O L Q T V O Z U
F M E L M D O E S N I P I U U X V Y
N K T J O N T M L D K C J S I G G E
Q U A R R E L E W D C V D A H E F B
H I E H G X F T R U T H G B F C G A
```

154

Find the words in the square (diagonal, up or down) that answer the following questions:

1. A false witness will not go _____ (Proverbs 19:5).
2. With what part of your body is it easiest to sin? _____
3. With his _____ the godless destroys his neighbor (Proverbs 11:9).
4. Man's _____ does not bring about the righteous life that God desires (James 1:20).
5. A quick-tempered man does _____ things (Proverbs 14:17).
6. Unless you give all your _____ to Jesus, you will never conquer anger.
7. A gentle answer turns away _____ (Proverbs 15:1).
8. A patient man calms a _____ (Proverbs 15:18).
9. He who loves a quarrel loves _____ (Proverbs 17:19).
10. Quarrels do not depend on issues but on _____ .
11. Out of the overflow of the _____ the mouth speaks (Matthew 12:34).
12. If you ignore some root of bitterness, it will grow and become a

   _____ .
13. A wicked man listens to evil _____ (Proverbs 17:4).
14. Keep falsehood and _____ far from me (Proverbs 30:8).
15. If you always speak the _____ , you'll be able to detect when the other person is lying.
16. Whoever flatters his neighbor is spreading a _____ for his feet (Proverbs 29:5).
17. The truth must always be spoken in _____ .
18. If you are a mocker, you alone will _____ (Proverbs 9:12).
19. Men _____ a mocker (Proverbs 24:9).
20. _____ company corrupts good character (1 Corinthians 15:33).
21. The tongue of the _____ brings healing (Proverbs 12:18).

The completed puzzle is on page 272.

ANSWERS: 1. unpunished. **2.** tongue. **3.** mouth. **4.** anger. **5.** foolish. **6.** rights. **7.** wrath. **8.** quarrel. **9.** sin. **10.** people. **11.** heart. **12.** monster. **13.** lips. **14.** lies. **15.** truth. **16.** net. **17.** love. **18.** suffer. **19.** detest. **20.** Bad. **21.** wise.

Part Four

The Fine Art of Getting Along With People

CHAPTER 27

When Parents Become Impossible

Casey's parents were very liberal, and Casey pretty much did as he pleased. In his family, "individual freedom" was a basic value, so there was little friction. On the other hand, none of the family members were very close.

Then everything changed. While Casey accepted Christ as his Savior, his parents became involved in a cult. Immediately they began to oppose almost everything Casey wanted to do. They forbade him to attend his friends' church, and even wrote for a church bulletin so they could monitor all his activities. Fortunately, they didn't know about the Christian club at school that met on Tuesday nights, so Casey managed to get some fellowship. But when his mom was cleaning his room, she found his Bible study material and tore it up. He got another workbook and hid it in a better place.

Since Casey had always been instructed to defend his freedom, he angrily accused his parents of going against the principles they'd taught him. That resulted in a nasty argument, which left Casey frustrated. Why was it that the Christian friends he'd made all had parents who encouraged them or just didn't care? He felt he'd been cheated.

When his friends told him about senior-high Bible camp, he really wanted to go. Since his parents were planning to travel out of state for a cult convention that very same week, he felt it was his perfect opportunity. Casey secretly made plans to get off work and go to Bible camp.

Before they left, however, his folks warned him specifically: "Don't attend any activities from that church while we're gone. If you disobey, you'll have to find another place to live." Casey made no reply. He couldn't imagine how they'd ever find out. There were no relatives nearby to answer to, and he could use the telephone answering machine to catch phone calls, should his parents check up on him.

As soon as his parents left, Casey quickly packed his suitcase.

The week was wonderful, almost like visiting heaven! There were great Bible studies, encouragement from other Christians, praise sessions, swimming and other sports, and a chance to enjoy some wilderness trails.

But the things the speaker said the last night made Casey very uneasy. "The Bible says, 'Children obey your parents.' It doesn't tell you to obey your parents *if* they are Christians, or *if* they are right, or *if* they are kind. It just says, 'Obey your parents' period.

"It's been my experience over the years that the young people who lovingly obeyed their non-Christian parents—even those who refused to let them go to the church of their choice—won them over to their side in the end. But it required them to be faithful in prayer."

He went on to say, "Proverbs 21:1 informs us, 'The king's heart is in the hand of the Lord; he directs it like a watercourse wherever he pleases.' If God could convince Pharaoh to let all the Israelites leave Egypt, He can certainly persuade your parents to permit you to attend church. When you argue, badger, and demand, *you* are in control, not God. You actually block the work of the Holy Spirit when you try to usurp His position—so things only get worse. God knows what you need. "If you *pray* and *obey*, letting God take charge, you'll be surprised at the results."

Casey asked God to forgive him for his rebellion against his parents. He determined to obey without giving them any flack in the future.

He wasn't quite prepared for the next round, though.

When he arrived home, his parents' car was in the driveway! He was flustered and fearful. Why did God allow him to get caught? What should he do?

➡ THIS WAY OUT ➡ ➡

🖎 Asking God to Meet Legitimate Needs

Dear God, you tell me to honor and obey my parents. Give me the correct attitudes. Right now I think my mom/dad is wrong in asking me to _____. Show me if I'm mistaken. And even if I'm right, I'm willing to obey anyway—but I ask you to change his/her heart.

🖎 Getting the Facts Straight

The king's heart is in the hand of the Lord; he directs it like a watercourse [small channel of water, as used in irrigation] wherever he pleases (Proverbs 21:1).

There is no wisdom, no insight, no plan that can succeed against the Lord. The horse is made ready for the day of battle, but victory rests with the Lord (Proverbs 21:30–31).

Many are the plans in a man's heart, but it is the Lord's purpose that prevails (Proverbs 19:21).

The Lord works out everything for his own ends—even the wicked for a day of disaster (Proverbs 16:4).

One of the most important things a Christian can learn is that God has everything under control and He is all-powerful. That is why you can obey a person in authority, even if he or she is wrong—unless it requires lying, stealing, denying Jesus or something else clearly forbidden in the Scriptures. This does not rule out appealing to the person in charge and *suggesting* a different approach.

On the "power" side, you can pray and ask God to change the heart of the person who is giving the unnecessary work, the wrong instructions, or the unreasonable rules. As you pray in faith, you'll realize that you are no longer a victim of injustice, foolishness, or cruelty. Because you are laying your petitions before the Lord, He *is* at work for you. Yes, it is possible to submit to authority and to wait patiently for God to act—realizing that no person, however strong he or she appears, can upset God's eternal plan.

It's also very helpful to know that God even uses evil to work out His good purposes. In the end, of course, the bad person will receive what he deserves, but God's plan will still go into operation. For instance, Hitler's murder of six million Jews moved almost all the countries in the United Nations to vote for the establishment of the Jewish State of Israel.

It is possible that you are suffering greatly because of the sins of your parents. Obeying, loving, honoring, and praying for them will keep you in constant reliance upon the supernatural power of God. Hang in there, and refuse to listen to Satan when he whispers, "Your case is so extreme that you have a right to ignore God's command to obey your parents." Someday you'll reap the benefits in your life!

↗ Rethinking the Situation

Casey found the front door locked. As he rang the doorbell he prayed, *"Lord, I'll be honest, and I'll submit to their authority."*

Both his mom and dad came to the door. "Casey, where were you?" his father demanded. "We've been worried about you."

"I have to tell you truth," Casey began. "I disregarded your instructions and went to the church Bible camp. It was so ironic, because I learned more about obeying my parents. Will you forgive me?"

Neither parent replied, and the next few days were lived in cold silence.

Casey did everything he could to help around the house. He didn't argue, or try to sneak off to church. Daily he prayed for his parents.

Although his folks shared little, Casey began to see that they were becoming unhappy with the cult they were involved in. Then one day they got the news that the seventeen-year-old son of their cult leaders had committed suicide. This really shook up his mother. The next evening she said simply, "Your father and I have discussed the matter. You're free to go to church, if that's what you want."

☞ Putting the Truth Into Practice

List the rules and attitudes of your teachers, your parents, and your boss which make your life difficult: _____

_____

_____

_____

_____

Determine that you will honor them, submit to their authority, and pray in faith that God will change them—and you!

If there is something sinful on the list, such as a teacher requiring your participation in an occult activity, prayerfully make your appeal. If it is denied, be prepared to accept the consequences of disobeying an order that is contrary to God's Word. Then pray for the authorities who give you the most trouble.

CHAPTER 28

Give Your Parents the Gift of Joy

Vanessa was discouraged when she returned home from Ashley's birthday party. *If only my parents were like hers,* she thought. Ashley's mother jogged to maintain her schoolgirl figure, kept up with the trends and dressed in style. Her father had a tremendous sense of humor and was popular with all of Ashley's friends. Their house could be featured in *Better Homes and Gardens* magazine.

Vanessa was ashamed of her house and her parents. It wasn't that they were poor; her father made good money. But her mom randomly bought the furniture she liked, whether or not it went together. And she definitely preferred the cluttered look. She still hung the pictures a foot from the ceiling, like they did in Mexico when she was a child. Besides her Spanish accent and poor grammar, she never really caught on to American ways. Her love for tortillas and fried food added extra pounds every year. She kissed Vanessa in public and still called her *Vanesita.*

Vanessa was the youngest of seven children and the only one still at home. Her father was determined to be strict with her so she wouldn't turn out like her older sister, who had run away from home. A retired army officer, he forgot that he was no longer in uniform and Vanessa wasn't a soldier. Staying out after 10:00 P.M., and accepting rides from guys were on his list of taboos. So Vanessa had a lot of arguments with her parents, and was becoming rebellious.

On the other hand, before Vanessa's parents had become Christians, her father drank a lot and her folks fought constantly, but now things were different. Vanessa had to admit that her parents loved each other and they loved her. But she was sure that with all their rules she would never live a normal life, never find a boyfriend and never get married. As she became more bitter, she blamed all her problems on her "old-fashioned" parents.

Vanessa was vivacious, the life of the party. Her jokes and impersonations were very popular with her friends. She began doing a "My Parents Belong in the Eighteenth Century" routine, which made fun of her folks, exaggerating a lot to add comedy. After one of her outstanding performances, though, she noticed that Landon had a serious expression.

"What's the matter?" she asked. "Didn't you like my show?"

"To be honest, I didn't," he replied. "You see, my parents are divorced. I haven't seen my father for five years. My mom lives with her boyfriend, who's an alcoholic and hates my guts. They go out to eat and drink every night. I always eat supper alone. It doesn't seem to me that your parents are all that bad. I wish somebody cared enough about me to make me obey some rules."

▼ ▼ ▼ THIS WAY OUT ▼ ▼ ▼

☛ Asking God to Meet Legitimate Needs

Dear God, because you used one of your Ten Commandments to tell me to honor my parents, I know it's very important to you. I also realize that you made all your rules for my good. Forgive me for not wanting to obey the mother and father you gave me. Right now I don't like them telling me to _____ . Help me to change my wrong attitudes, and to be willing to submit to their authority.

🖊 Getting the Facts Straight

If a man curses his father or mother, his lamp will be snuffed out in pitch darkness (Proverbs 20:20).

Listen to your father, who gave you life, and do not despise your mother when she is old. Buy the truth and do not sell it; get wisdom, discipline and understanding. The father of a righteous man has great joy; he who has a wise son delights in him. May your father and mother be glad; may she who gave you birth rejoice! (Proverbs 23:22–25).

The eye that mocks a father, that scorns obedience to a mother, will be pecked out by the ravens of the valley, will be eaten by the vultures (Proverbs 30:17).

The Devil is a master deceiver. He has successfully hoodwinked generations of teenagers into thinking they know more than their parents, and that they are perfectly within their "rights" to disobey "out-moded" rules and "old-fashioned" ideas. Society considers this normal. But disobeying God's command to honor one's parents is not par for the course, and it's not to be excused by saying, "Times have changed." *It is sin.*

The Bible specifically tells you, "Despise not your mother when she is old." What would your home be like if your parents were suddenly transformed into full-fledged teenagers? In that case, you'd probably do almost anything to turn them back into their reliable, consistent, older generation selves! A car needs both an engine and brakes. At your house most likely you and your brothers and sisters are the engine and your parents are the brakes. Thank God for the brakes! Respect them and honor them for their position—and *love* them, even when they unnecessarily pull the emergency brake.

Receive God's grace to honor and accept your parents, despite their idiosyncrasies and faults. Learning to love your parents despite their failures is the best preparation for life. Those who fail to pass this test don't learn to respect authority, and their constant discontent brings misery both to themselves and to others.

It's boring to always just get by, and Proverbs has a formula for turning duty into delight. You are to rise above the minimum standard of submitting to parental authority and to become a joy to your father and your mother. Do everything possible to make them happy. If you decide to really work at loving and serving your parents, you're investing in changing your family for the better.

✔ Rethinking the Situation

What Landon said really made Vanessa start thinking. She'd never realized how much she had to be thankful for. Then one night she found a startling verse in Proverbs: "The eye that mocks a father, that scorns obedience to a mother will be pecked out by the ravens of the valley, will be eaten by the vultures." *Wow!* she thought, *It looks like it's dangerous for me to make fun of my parents. And what I say about them certainly isn't honoring.*

On the spot, Vanessa bowed her head, and prayed for forgiveness. Then she asked God how she should tell her parents she was sorry. A wonderful idea occurred to her. She decided to use the money she had saved up to invite them out to eat at a nice restaurant.

After explaining her plan to her parents, she noticed that they looked happier than she'd seen them for a long time.

On the evening of their "date," her mom wore her best dress. Vanessa looked at her parents across the candlelit table.

"I invited you here," she began, "to tell you that I'm sorry for the way I've been acting. I'd like to thank you for all you've done for me. I love you very much."

Her mother started to cry, and her father had tears in his eyes, too. Finally he said, "I'll always remember this night as one of the most special times of my whole life."

✔ Putting the Truth Into Practice

"May your father and mother be glad" (Proverbs 23:25).

Decide to do everything you can to put joy into the lives of your parents. Make a list of the things that will make your father and mother happy. Give them the gift of joy.

Actions: _____

_____

_____

_____

Attitudes: _____

_____

_____

Responses to their requests and words that express encouragement, love and appreciation: _____

_____

_____

_____

_____

Put at least one of these ways of honoring your parents into action every day for a month and see what it does in your home.

CHAPTER 29

The Love Experiment

Britta was a quiet, pretty girl, sensitive to the feelings of others. And she was a sincere Christian. Like all the other kids from her church, she was excited about the upcoming Saturday ski trip, to be followed by pizza and hot chocolate and a youth rally in the church basement.

Britta's father had promised to drive her to the ski area, but Friday night he found out that an emergency sales meeting had been called for Saturday morning.

"Just call up Nathan and tell him you need a ride," her father advised. "I'm sure it won't be a problem. I don't want you riding with Marty. He drives like a maniac."

Because Nathan, the new seminary student in charge of the youth, was young, single, and good-looking, Britta hesitated. She didn't want it to look like she was chasing him. So her mother phoned Nathan instead, and then turned the phone over to Britta so they could make the final arrangements.

"I'd be glad to pick you up, Britta," Nathan said amiably. "I'll be there at 8:00 A.M. sharp."

Britta got up early and was ready long before 8:00. She propped her skis up against the wall on the porch and had everything else laid out in the entry way. Then she sat down to read a magazine. When 8:30 rolled around, there was still no sign of Nathan. At 9:00 her mother called his apartment and there was no answer. At 10:00 Britta finally took off her ski clothes and started on her weekend home-work—feeling miserable!

Somehow the account in her history book of the administration of Woodrow Wilson kept being interrupted by feelings of rejection, disappointment, and anger. Why did Nathan promise to pick her up, and then forget about her? Maybe he thought she called just to try to trap him, and he wanted to teach her a lesson. But then, why didn't he just tell her *no*? Thinking about all the fun everyone else was having made her even more depressed.

Her mom was quick to catch Britta's mood. As soon as her dad got home with the car, she promised to drive her to Pine Crest.

Britta was on the slopes by 1:15. When Nathan saw her waiting in a lift line, he smiled nonchalantly, "Oh! I was supposed to pick you up, wasn't I?" he said casually. "I'm sorry. I had so much on my mind that I forgot. I'm glad you made it on your own."

Britta thought, *If my broken promise caused someone to miss a half day of skiing, I'd apologize as if I really meant it.* Although she felt bad, she decided to try to enjoy the rest of the day. And she was almost recuperating when she rode up the chair lift with her friend, Erin. "You know what Nichole is saying about you?" Erin fumed.

"No, what?" Britta responded.

"She told everyone that you have a crush on Nathan, so you tried to make him take you skiing even though it's obvious you had transportation. And she's saying that Nathan didn't stop by for you because he thinks you're a big flirt."

Britta was stunned. How could she just make up a story like that? It was common knowledge that *Nichole* liked Nathan—big time! All this added up to a ruthless attempt to destroy any "competition."

Britta started to cry. She just wanted to go home. What if everyone really believed Nichole? Perhaps the grapevine had already relayed the information to Nathan. Maybe that's why his apology was so lame.

Then it was as if the Devil started whispering in her ear: *What are you doing in this youth group anyway? The leader treats you second-rate, and a girl who's a regular spreads untrue gossip about you. Now everybody's talking behind your back. Just stop attending. That'll teach everyone a thing or two.*

▼ ▼ ▼ THIS WAY OUT ▼ ▼ ▼

☑ Asking God to Meet Legitimate Needs

Getting rid of bitterness, resentment, grudges, and hurt feelings is essential to healthy emotions—and to living the Christian life. There are two paths you can take to reach this goal, and both begin with totally forgiving the person who sinned against you. One is acknowledging your hurt only to God and letting Him heal you directly. Other times it is wise to lovingly tell the person who offended you what is bothering you so you can clear the air. (But don't keep mentioning it over and over.) Ask God which method is appropriate in each case.

Dear God, you know that _____ hurt me a lot when he/she said/did _____ .
I choose to forgive _____ . Please heal the pain I feel.
Show me if it would be wise to kindly confront _____ in order to avoid future problems. Help me not to hold a grudge or to rehash the situation endlessly in my mind.

☑ Getting the Facts Straight

A man of knowledge uses words with restraint, and a man of understanding is even-tempered (Proverbs 17:27).

A man's wisdom gives him patience; it is his glory to overlook an offense (Proverbs 19:11).

He who covers over an offense promotes love, but whoever repeats the matter separates close friends (Proverbs 17:9).

Hatred stirs up dissension, but love covers over all wrongs (Proverbs 10:12).

As humans, it's just not in us to give up a chance to get back at another person who has treated us unfairly, or to overlook ugly words. We've developed dozens of methods to get even with those who hurt us. Exploding in anger, crying a lot, giving the "cold shoulder," a dose of the silent treatment, letting everyone else know that Joe or Joanna is a rat, or spreading a rumor to even the score—these are only a few of the options. And they all backfire, because the recipient of our revenge usually uses some stored up ammunition of his or her own to retaliate.

To break this vicious cycle, we need the love and forgiveness of Jesus. You can experience the caring touch of Jesus and the freedom that comes in knowing "the blood of Jesus purifies us from all sin" (1 John 1:7).

Our *willingness* to forgive and forget forms the fountain through which the supernatural love of Jesus can flow out to those around us— even our enemies. It is a *glory* to overlook an offense, and that glory is receiving the love of Jesus so we can pass it on. Love covers all wrongs and a multitude of sins. Besides that, it promotes more love, changing a vicious cycle into an ever-widening sphere of respect and acceptance.

If you've never permitted the supernatural love of Jesus to melt your resentments and wipe out your grudges, try this new experiment—you'll love the results.

☑ Rethinking the Situation

Britta automatically got off the chair lift and started down the hill. It was a gorgeous afternoon, and the view from the summit was breathtaking. She couldn't help thinking that God had done a really neat job when He created this section of planet earth. This break in her vengeful thoughts gave the Holy Spirit a chance to bring a Bible verse to her mind: "But if you do not forgive men their sins, your father will not forgive your sins" (Matthew 6:15).

Britta had had enough experience with God to know that if she was willing to love and forgive, God would enable her to carry out her intentions.

When she reached the bottom of the hill she stopped for a short prayer. She gave her hurt feelings to God and asked for His healing. She declared her willingness to forgive Nathan and Nichole. And she asked God for His love for them.

The next time down the slope, she came up on Nichole, who had hit a patch of ice and taken a nasty fall. In an instant, Britta was by her side comforting her and praying for her. She accompanied Nichole in the ambulance and stayed by her side until her parents arrived at the hospital. By that time Nathan had found out what happened and had come to see how Nichole was doing.

When Nichole found out that her broken leg required immediate surgery, she turned to Britta. "I have something to confess," she began. Obviously in pain and fighting tears, she stammered, "I spread the rumor that you were chasing Nathan and so you made up the story that you needed a ride to Pine Crest. I told everyone that Nathan forgot you on purpose because he was fed up with your flirting. And after all that, you're the one who showed me so much love and gave up skiing to come with me to the hospital. I'm so ashamed. Will you forgive me?" she pleaded.

"I already have," smiled Britta.

Later on, Nathan also sought out Britta. "I need to ask your forgiveness," he said. "I totally forgot, honest I did. I'd be glad to give you a ride anytime you need one."

Britta thought, *God's love works the nicest miracles.*

✔️ Putting the Truth Into Practice

THE LOVE EXPERIMENT

1. Have you already used God's love to melt an enemy? If so, recall your experience.

2. Who are your prime candidates for the "love experiment" right now? _____ _____ , _____ , __

   a. Pray for them daily.
   b. Forgive them totally. If God leads you to talk to one of them about the problem, do so *once* and do it with a loving attitude.
   c. Ask God for good ideas on how to show love to these people.

CHAPTER 30

Letting God's Faithfulness Rub Off on You!

Ryan was a born salesman—personable, outgoing, smooth, and convincing. When he joined a Christian group on campus that strongly emphasized witnessing, he became an instant star.

Sharing his faith came easy, and Ryan boldly testified to anyone who would listen. He took advantage of each opportunity that presented itself in the classroom. When Spanish III students had to give short speeches in Spanish, he spoke on how to receive Christ as your Savior and even quoted four Bible verses in Spanish.

Joel admired Ryan—he always seemed to be able to witness with a flair. Shy and less verbal, Joel had a harder time sharing the deep faith he had in Jesus. Joel, however, was a guy you could always count on. He handed in every homework assignment, went to the hospital twice a week to see a classmate who was recovering from a broken back, and spent time in Bible study and prayer every day.

Ryan was more nonchalant. He was smart enough to pull off decent grades by cramming at the last minute, so he studied only in spurts. Often late, he saw no need to apologize. He charmed his way out of keeping promises or serving on committees that required hard work.

Miss Tucker, the Spanish III teacher, had just graduated from college and she had a lot of creative ideas for giving her students an opportunity to use the language. She arranged for her pupils to put on parties for the children in the barrio who as yet spoke no English. Joel served faithfully on the invitation committee, and even though no one else showed up, he went door-to-door inviting the children.

Excited boys and girls showed up at the park on the day of the picnic. Students interviewed each child and the games went well— until it was discovered that Ryan forgot to buy the piñata. Ryan's charm and his excuses didn't cut it this time.

Determined to regain Miss Tucker's favor, Ryan told her he could get a 40% discount for the class at the best Mexican restaurant in town if they went on a Tuesday night. And so she let him arrange for dinner at Rivera's.

At 6:00 P.M. on Tuesday, everyone entered the room reserved for them and sat down at the candlelit tables. The teacher explained each menu item and insisted that the students speak to the waiters in Spanish. Everyone learned something, and they had a lot of fun. When it came time to pay the bill, however, neither the waiters nor the night manager had heard anything about a 40% discount. Ryan called the owner at his home, and discovered that the special discount was given only to groups of fifty or more who had advance reservations and all ordered the same menu item.

When he returned from making the phone call, Ryan tried to place blame on the owner, but his classmates were really upset. Miss Tucker exploded: "I'm sick and tired of religious fanatics who lie and don't keep promises!" she screamed. "I don't know what a guy like Joel believes, but I'd like to find out. He's the only student who has never let me down."

◆ ◆ ◆ THIS WAY OUT ◆ ◆ ◆

☑️ Asking God to Meet Legitimate Needs

Dear God, I know that your Word says, "Now it is required that those who have been given a trust must prove faithful" (1 Corin-

thians 4:2). But I'm getting bored and restless. Help me to be faithful in doing my schoolwork, in helping around the house, and in cleaning my room. Make me into a person who keeps promises and is reliable. I'll cooperate with you. _____ *and* _____ *are specific problems right now. Show me how I can learn faithfulness in these areas.*

▶ Getting the Facts Straight

Many a man claims to have unfailing love, but a faithful man who can find? (Proverbs 20:6).

Like the coolness of snow at harvest time is a trustworthy messenger to those who send him; he refreshes the spirit of his masters (Proverbs 25:13).

A faithful man will be richly blessed (Proverbs 28:20).

Like clouds and wind without rain is a man who boasts of gifts he does not give (Proverbs 25:14).

Like a bad tooth or a lame foot is reliance on the unfaithful in times of trouble (Proverbs 25:19).

When was the last time that someone you really trusted let you down? The memory is a painful one. If the person who failed to live up to his word was a Christian, the situation is even more difficult. It's hard to separate an individual from his or her message. Even though all of us know that Jesus is perfect and God's Word is sure, if the person from whom we first learned about faith in Christ fails us it's a severe blow. If you're suffering because of someone's faithlessness, it's important that you forgive him/her and then place total trust in Jesus, the only One who will never disappoint you.

It's also wise to consider the effect that your own faithfulness—or lack of it—will have on others. If you didn't pay someone the money you owe, then that friend won't be interested in hearing about how Jesus has changed your life. When you keep someone waiting at the restaurant forty-five minutes, that person might not be impressed by the fact that you bow your head and give thanks before eating. The aunt who never received thank-you notes for the Christmas presents she gave you is not likely to read the tract you send her. Talking big and doing little is not the way to win the world for Jesus.

On the other hand, there are "faithfulness investments" you can make in other people. Your constant attitude of respect will be noticed by your teacher. Doing extra work without being told will make your boss wonder why you're different. Being the first to help a person in need demonstrates the love of Jesus. Determine that faithfulness will characterize your life.

⚑ Rethinking the Situation

Miss Tucker's words kept coming back to Ryan, "I'm sick and tired of religious fanatics who lie and don't keep promises." Finally, he decided to talk with Greg, his Bible study leader. Greg listened carefully as Ryan told him everything that had happened.

"I like a story I once heard," Greg began, "in which a man asked his pastor, 'Which part of my witness is most important, my words or my life?' The pastor replied, 'Which wing of an airplane is most important, the right or left?' If our lives don't match our testimony, we turn people off. But if we only live a good life and say nothing, we never turn them on.

"I've watched you, Ryan. You come from a family in which details and keeping your word, no matter what, aren't so important. You're used to letting things slide, getting out of work when possible, shirking responsibility, and covering it all up with charm. You use the "love 'em and leave 'em" approach to evangelism. You're very weak on follow-up. All these things indicate that you need to build faithfulness into your life."

"What should I do about it?" Ryan wanted to know. "I'm not even sure where to start."

"Right now, what is your eight-hour-a-day prime responsibility?" Greg questioned.

"Well, school, I guess," Ryan returned.

"So you start there," Greg said firmly. "Study consistently, hand in all your homework, and keep all your promises to your teachers. Next, work on faithfulness at home—obeying your parents, and fulfilling your responsibilities around the house. Then decide never to make a promise to a friend that you're not sure you can keep."

"I guess it's pretty simple," Ryan admitted. "It just means that I can't get out of anything."

"And you've got Jesus to help you," Greg reminded. "He's always by your side. When you go into partnership with Him, His faithfulness will rub off on you."

☛ Putting the Truth Into Practice

FAITHFULNESS QUESTIONNAIRE
(Circle True or False)

1. If I say that I'll pick someone up, I keep my word.   T   F
2. I'm almost always on time.   T   F
3. If I promise to send a letter for someone, I make it a point to find a mailbox immediately.   T   F
4. I wouldn't be guilty of sticking the letter in with my school papers, then make a frantic search a month later when I bump into a mailbox, only to discover that I've lost it.   T   F
5. I can't think of any broken promises I've made to my brothers and sisters, or nieces and nephews.   T   F
6. I never lie to the kids I baby-sit for, to keep them off my back.   T   F
7. If I tell my mom I'll clean my room, I do it.   T   F
8. Procrastinating isn't one of my bad habits.   T   F
9. I hand in all my homework on time.   T   F
10. I usually answer letters within a reasonable length of time.   T   F
11. I don't exaggerate when I tell others what I did.   T   F

Whoever can be trusted with very little can also be trusted with much, and whoever is dishonest with very little will also be dishonest with much (Luke 16:10).

Well done, good and faithful servant! You have been faithful with a few things; I will put you in charge of many things (Matthew 25:23).

If you honestly answered the questions above, the number of T's you circled indicates something of how much responsibility God will be able to entrust to you in the future. And remember, if you need to change: Jesus is willing to help you keep your word, take responsibility, and faithfully execute the details of your life.

CHAPTER 31

It's Either Good or Grief!

Beth and Bridget were sisters and they looked a lot alike: Each had beautiful, big brown eyes, a clear complexion, curly hair, and a short, stocky build. But here the similarity ended.

Bridget resented her dad for leaving the family for another woman two years before. She was jealous of her mother who was shapely and slender, even at age forty-two. She often commented, "It's just my luck to be fat like my father." She felt like life hadn't given her a fair shake. Since she never was able to break into the popular girls' circle, she spent her time ridiculing them and rejoicing in their failures. She believed that one bad turn deserves another, and unleashed her revenge against those who dared to defy her. Because they didn't want to listen to constant complaining, people avoided her, and that gave her a new reason to gripe. She was good at broadcasting the faults of others and usually had something negative to say.

Beth, on the other hand, decided to give God her whole life and to really believe that He could work good out of evil. She remembered hearing, "Everything—no matter how horrible—has been filtered through God's hands by the time it touches you. And He already has a plan to turn it to good, if you trust and obey Him." So she loved and accepted her father in spite of what he'd done. She believed that God had a unique plan for creating her just the way she was. She determined not to waste time comparing herself with others. Asking God each day for *His* love for others, she was cheerful and kind to most everyone—even to those who didn't treat her right. Her positive attitude attracted many friends.

On the week of Bridget's birthday, their mom left for a business convention in New Orleans. Beth bought a cake and gave Bridget a nice present—but Bridget didn't hide her disappointment about not being given a party.

177

Two months later, on Beth's birthday, her friends all came over bringing a huge cake, pizza and presents. The contrast vividly showed the differences in their social lives. Beth always had places to go and people to do things with, while Bridget sat home and made fun of Beth's "religious fanatic" friends.

To make matters worse, Bridget spent all her money on make-up and clothes, but nobody seemed to notice. All Beth needed to do was to put on a new blouse and she received compliments galore.

But the final blow came when Beth started dating Matthew, a really sharp, good-looking guy. Bridget was furious, *How could my sister land a guy like that when I can't? She and I look so much alike that everyone thinks we're twins. Besides, my clothes are nicer and I even took a course on how to put on make-up.* She thought about ways to break them up—but knew that would not solve her problem.

◆ ◆ ◆ THIS WAY OUT ◆ ◆ ◆

☛ Asking God to Meet Legitimate Needs

Learning to thank God for *everything* and to trust His purposes when circumstances seem to be totally out of control is absolutely necessary if you are going to live a contented and victorious Christian life. But you'll have to truly look for good in every situation or you'll never find it.

Dear God, thank you that you're in control of everything, even

_____. *Teach me the importance of constantly giving thanks. Show me how to seek for the best in everything and to look on the bright side. Forgive me for griping and complaining about _____. I know that grumbling is sin.*

✔ Getting the Facts Straight

He who seeks good finds goodwill, but evil comes to him who searches for it (Proverbs 11:27).

A kind man benefits himself, but a cruel man brings trouble on himself (Proverbs 11:17).

The desire of the righteous ends only in good, but the hope of the wicked only in wrath (Proverbs 11:23).

Delight yourself in the Lord and he will give you the desires of your heart (Psalms 37:4).

Whoever gloats over disaster will not go unpunished (Proverbs 17:5).

The ultimate reward for righteousness and punishment for sin will come in the life after death. But you'll reap what you sow in this life, as well. The consequences of your decisions *will* determine the course of your life.

Take time to think about this: Your life is not an accident. You *choose* your attitudes, your friends, and your activities. Without the supernatural power of the Holy Spirit, which is available only to Christians, you cannot make the very best choices. God will not *force* you to do what is right. And so many Christian young people, with all the resources Christ offers for successful living, permit lax attitudes and sin to drag them down along with everyone else.

Proverbs maintains that the person "who seeks good finds goodwill." But constantly looking for excellence and justice takes work, persistence, and willingness to be different from the rest. Dropping a positive comment into a group of complainers means instant ostracism.

"Seeking good" means maintaining an unwavering faith in God, who works out all things for good.

The story is told of an old man who often stood out by the trail as wagon trains of settlers pressed westward. One day a man stopped and asked, "What kind of people will I find on the other side of the mountains?"

"What kind of neighbors did you have back East?" the old gentleman wanted to know.

"They were unfriendly, selfish and mean," replied the pioneer.

"You'll find the same kind of folk on the other side of the mountains," the old gent predicted.

At the end of the same wagon train, a second homesteader asked the same question, and again the old man asked about his neighbors back East.

This man affirmed that his neighbors had always been hospitable, generous, faithful and kind.

Then the old man told him, "The people who live on the other side of the mountains are just the same!"

You too, will find what you look for. The teen who has no Christian friends didn't search hard enough. The person who has nothing positive to say really finds criticizing more enjoyable. It takes work and discipline to seek for good.

📝 Rethinking the Situation

Bridget was in her pajamas late one evening when Beth and Matthew approached the front door. Her only escape was to hide in the coat closet.

"You and Bridget are *so* different," Matthew was saying as they walked in. "I just can't believe you're sisters."

"If only I could get Bridget to see that she needs Jesus," Beth replied. "If she could just understand that God has a purpose in everything. I've been able to help a lot of other kids whose parents are divorced. I wish my own sister could see that God especially designed each of us to fit into His plan! Bridget is really a very neat person, but the chip she carries on her shoulder hides all that."

The words brought tears to Bridget's eyes and conviction to her heart. She wanted what Beth had. In the darkness, she could feel the stylish raincoat she'd just bought. She put it on and decided to come out of the closet—both literally and figuratively. When the raincoated figure popped out of the closet, Beth and Matthew were startled—then burst into laughter.

"I do want Jesus to change my life, like He's changed yours," Bridget approached the topic hesitantly. "Will you guys help me?"

There and then, Bridget invited Jesus into her life. She confessed her bitterness, and prayed for help to act like the new creature she had just become.

☑ **Putting the Truth Into Practice**

TREASURE HUNT

List the good in these people and situations. Thank God for the positive things you find:

Good Points

Mother	Father	Brothers and Sisters

Teachers	Leaders and Bosses	Friends

The good side of things I complain about most:

_____

_____

_____

_____

MEMORIZE: "Always giving thanks to God the Father for everything, in the name of our Lord Jesus Christ" (Ephesians 5:20).

CHAPTER 32

Andy's Secret

Mike wanted to be a strong testimony in his new high school. He wasn't ashamed of Jesus and he'd been taught never to miss an opportunity to witness.

One day Mr. Barnhardt, the biology teacher, started his lesson with, "Now all educated people accept evolution as a fact."

Mike raised his hand. "Evolution is contrary to the Bible. I'd rather believe God, and be thought ignorant by the world. You can call me what you like, but your college degree won't get you to heaven."

At this, Mr. Barnhardt began to ridicule Mike, and the class laughed.

During lunch, Mike cornered a guy who was sitting alone and told him he'd go to hell if he didn't accept Jesus. Although the fellow said he wasn't interested, Mike insisted on finishing his message.

By sixth hour his reputation had gotten around. A kid in the locker room pretended to be interested in the Bible and as Mike delivered his evangelistic message, everybody gave him a hard time. He finished his sermon, though, satisfied that he was "suffering for Jesus."

Soon everybody ignored him, and teachers made it a point never to call on him.

One day in social studies class, there was a debate on abortion. Andy, one of the top students in the class, was taking a position against it. He had prepared well, and gave a lot of statistics. When he presented the biblical view of the sacredness of life, everyone listened with respect. Mike was shocked. Andy had so many friends, he never suspected him of being a Christian.

About two months later, when the biology teacher again affirmed that no intelligent person could doubt evolution, Andy raised his hand. "Isn't scientific fact based on experimental evidence, which always gives the same results when reproduced under similar conditions?" he asked.

"Yes," replied the teacher. "Why?"

"Because it's impossible to arrange even one respectable experiment to prove the transition of one species of life to another. That means evolution is a *theory*, not a fact—correct?" pressed Andy.

"But any idiot knows it's more scientific than Adam and Eve and the snake," scoffed Mr. Barnhardt.

"It seems to me—laying all prejudice aside," Andy continued, "that both ideas require a lot of faith. There's no movie to show us how the world began. No detailed eyewitness account. No way of scientifically proving what happened. For me, it takes more faith to assume that something inanimate, like energy, accidentally produced life than to believe that a God who always existed created the universe."

"You're welcome to your opinion," the instructor replied. "I prefer to be enlightened."

"To me," Andy went on, "the biggest problem with the theory of evolution is its social implications. If I'm just a chance combination of atoms, with no eternity to look forward to, why bother? Maybe I should act like the animal I am. But if God really created me with a purpose, it's worth doing what's right—and I have something to live for."

The biology teacher had no answer. Mike noticed that the same kids who had laughed at him were favorably impressed. What was Andy's secret?

✦ ✦ ✦ THIS WAY OUT ✦ ✦ ✦

☛ Asking God to Meet Legitimate Needs

Dear God, just because some people lack tact and common sense in their witnessing is no excuse for me to keep quiet. I know that your Word says, "But in your hearts set apart Christ as Lord. Always be prepared to give an answer to everyone who asks you to give the reason for the hope that you have. But do this with gentleness and respect" (1 Peter 3:15). Lord, teach me to be sensitive and appropriate at all times—but especially when I'm talking about the most important Person in the whole world.

☛ Getting the Facts Straight

If a man loudly blesses his neighbor early in the morning, it will be taken as a curse (Proverbs 27:14).

Let your conversation be always full of grace, seasoned with salt, so that you may know how to answer everyone (Colossians 4:6).

"She means well, but. . . "; "He has a good heart, but I can't stand to be around him for long." You've heard statements like these. There are some ways to make sure that the person making these comments isn't referring to you!

In conversations, take time to find out where the other person is coming from, so you can choose your words and chart your actions accordingly. This *always* requires more listening than speaking. A sad person needs understanding—not a lecture on praising the Lord. If someone has doubts about God's existence, one sentence directed toward that issue will do more good than presenting the entire plan of salvation. If you come to give a follow-up lesson to a new Christian who is totally bummed out about a geometry assignment, explaining the homework will be more beneficial than trying to preach to a person who's too upset to concentrate. Find out if the guy likes sports before inviting him to the football game, and keep the girl on a diet away from the all-you-can-eat special.

Some people give useless gifts, insist on helping us with things we'd rather do ourselves, and present us with lots of information that has nothing to do with our situation. Before you give "trinkets" of advice, spiritual instruction or help, find out what the person *needs*. People can live without pre-fab counseling, pre-recorded prayers and pre-packaged presents.

Spend so much time with Jesus that His graciousness and appropriateness rub off on you. Notice how naturally He related to people's needs. He displayed calmness, peace, joy, and purpose in His ministry. When you truly rely on the Holy Spirit to show you what Jesus would have you say or do at the moment, your actions and words will fit the situation.

◤ Rethinking the Situation

After school Mike was waiting at Andy's locker. "How come everybody listens when you speak out for Jesus and they laugh at me?" he asked abruptly.

"Let's go for a Coke so we can talk for a while," Andy suggested. At a little restaurant near school, they found a back booth and sat down.

"It's kind of like this," Andy explained. "Obeying God is a little like baking a cake. The end result is affected by changing or leaving out only one ingredient. I remember the time my mom put chili powder in her cake instead of cinnamon! It was a good-looking cake but no one could eat it.

"You're obeying a lot of God's commands about sharing your faith. You have boldness and you really want your fellow students to accept Christ. There's a reason why people take your intended blessings as curses—you're just not very sensitive to others."

Mike remained silent for a while. Finally he spoke: "Are you saying I'm presenting my message at inappropriate times and in the wrong way, so that the good news of Jesus isn't appreciated?"

"You've got it," Andy affirmed. "Jesus didn't interrupt people, force himself on them, or speak to those who weren't interested. Sometimes His introduction was only a few sentences, but it was enough to establish rapport. He didn't run around giving a canned speech to anyone He could buttonhole."

Andy paused, and then continued. "Jesus also said, 'Let your light shine before men, that they may see your good deeds and praise your Father in heaven' (Matthew 5:16). I wanted to witness to Mr. Barnhardt, but I knew he had a bad impression of Christians. So I had to gain his respect before I could say a word. I studied for every test, handed in each assignment, and even volunteered to help set up the science fair.

"And I also prayed for Mr. Barnhardt and for a chance to refute his lies in a way that wouldn't offend him. I asked the Holy Spirit to provide the right opening, because I realized that rushing ahead of God is just as bad as refusing to speak for Him. I also prayed for just the right words, because I know that certain terms set off a reaction in Mr. Barnhardt. I asked God to give me His opportunity and He answered my prayer."

"*Wow!*" exclaimed Mike. "I've got a lot to learn."

☛ Putting the Truth Into Practice

Are your good intentions sometimes interpreted as curses? There are some biblical principles that can change this. They can help you share your faith more effectively, favorably impress members of the opposite sex, maintain better relationships with authority figures, and become a better friend.

1. Practice being a good listener. ("He who answers before listening—that is his folly and his shame." Proverbs 18:13.)
2. Don't interrupt, or hog the conversation. ("Honor one another above yourselves." Romans 12:10.)
3. Don't put down another person, even if they're wrong and you know more about the subject. ("Do not be proud, but be willing to associate with people of low position. Do not be conceited." Romans 12:16.)
4. Become interested in the things the other person wishes to talk about. ("Each of you should look not only to your own interests, but also to the interests of others." Philippians 2:4.)
5. Maintain a positive attitude, even when everything is going wrong. ("Do everything without complaining or arguing." Philippians 2:14.)
6. Avoid arguments. ("Blessed are the peacemakers, for they will be called sons of God." Matthew 5:9.)

Make a chart like the one on the next page with enough space to last a month. Write down what you did each week in order to work on each of these problem areas:

Example

Learning to listen	Avoiding interrupting or talking too much	Practicing humility
I listened to Grandma tell stories of her youth. She enjoyed it and I learned some new things about her.	I caught myself interrupting, so I let Tammie finish.	I let George, our neighbor, tell me how to fix my car, even though I take automechanics and know more than he does.
Learning new interests	Keeping a positive attitude	Avoiding arguments
I asked Mrs. Mattson about her hobby, and learned all about quilting.	When my mom lost her car keys and we had to wait until my dad got back from golfing to leave from the shopping center, I tried to cheer her up and said I could watch the football game better on the 50 T.V. sets in the store than on only one at home.	When my mother angrily accused me of eating the last of the ice cream, I let her cool down before calmly explaining my innocence.

CHAPTER 33

Besides, God's Principles Really Work

Although Rob and Kirk weren't close friends, circumstances constantly put them together. They attended the same church and the same high school, and after filling out several applications for a part-time job, Rob got a call from the grocery store where Kirk worked. He showed up on Saturday ready to bag groceries.

The cashier with whom he was working was patient and helpful. Even though he made a lot of mistakes, she didn't lose her cool. But obviously Carol, the cashier at her side, *was* having a bad day, and she took it out on Kirk. When she told him in an impatient voice that oranges were heavier than apples and should be placed at the bottom of the bag, Kirk just smiled and said, "Okay." He cheerfully did his work and made friendly comments to the customers.

When a lady got angry because of an error Carol made, she blamed it on Kirk. "Your constant chattering makes me nervous," she complained. Kirk made no reply, and continued working hard.

At six o'clock Rob and Kirk left together. "How do you stand working under that woman?" Rob asked.

"I just figure I'm working for God," Kirk answered, "and He sees what I do. Besides, she has a lot of problems. Nobody cares for her. Maybe I'll send her a Christmas card."

The next Saturday Rob was assigned to work with Carol. When she criticized his work, Rob shot back, "I know what I'm doing. If something is wrong, I want the manager to correct it, not you." The exchange of put-downs continued throughout the day, and by midafternoon Carol had to go home with a migraine headache. Rob was blamed for it.

Carol's replacement got on Rob's case because he worked so slowly, and a customer came back to complain about two broken eggs.

This got Rob in trouble with the manager, and Rob joined the group of employees who constantly complained about the boss.

Meanwhile, Kirk was offered a bigger salary. His new position meant working Sundays, though. He thanked the manager and explained that he didn't think he should miss church because of his job. But after another month, the boss was so impressed with Kirk that he was promoted, with the promise of getting every Sunday off.

Then Mr. Elliot, the owner of the store, invited all the employees to his home for a Christmas party. Rob decided to make the most of his opportunity to impress the top brass. He initiated a conversation and filled it with flattery, then made references to his own great potential. But Mr. Elliot excused himself and went over to Kirk. "I've heard wonderful things about you, young man," he complimented. "I hope you'll consider staying with the store after you graduate from high school." Kirk smiled easily and thanked him for the offer.

Mrs. Elliot had done some baking for the party, including German chocolate cake and cherry tarts. Rob's mom never had time to bake, so he decided this was his chance to pig out. Getting in line first, he took two pieces of cake and three tarts.

As he was filling his plate for the third time, Mrs. Elliot commented, "I can't believe you, young man. Didn't you eat anything else today?"

Then she started talking to Kirk and took a special liking to him. "I noticed that we ran out of eggnog by the time you passed through the line. I never thought the store would sell out so fast. Here, I'd like to give you a little package of goodies for your break tomorrow."

By this time Rob was upset. Why did everyone prefer *Kirk* to him? He just couldn't figure it out.

THIS WAY OUT

✔ Asking God to Meet Legitimate Needs

Dear God, I know that Proverbs 22:29 says, "Do you see a man skillful in his work? He will serve before kings; he will not serve before obscure men." I want to become a good worker. Help me to have the right attitude toward each job I undertake. Show me how to serve my boss. Help me to apply myself so I learn to do each task well. I want to honor you and the people I work for.

✔ Getting the Facts Straight

A king's rage is like the roar of a lion, but his favor is like dew on the grass (Proverbs 19:12).

He who loves a pure heart and whose speech is gracious will have the king for his friend (Proverbs 22:11).

When you sit to dine with a ruler, note well what is before you, and put a knife to your throat if you are given to gluttony. Do not crave his delicacies, for that food is deceptive (Proverbs 23:1–3).

Fear the Lord and the king, my son, and do not join with the rebellious, for those two will send sudden destruction upon them, and who knows what calamities they can bring? (Proverbs 24:21–22).

Do not exalt yourself in the king's presence, and do not claim a place among great men; it is better for him to say to you, "Come up here," than for him to humiliate you before a nobleman (Proverbs 25:6–7).

Through patience a ruler can be persuaded, and a gentle tongue can break a bone (Proverbs 25:15).

Learning to please your teachers and your boss is extremely important. Many people hate their jobs and spend eight miserable hours each day because they've never learned to put into practice what Proverbs has to say about relating to your boss. If you acquire the heart of a servant and wholeheartedly put yourself into your work, you'll receive favor rather than rage from those for whom you work. If you learn this lesson as a young person, you'll save yourself a lot of trouble.

Unless your boss is Fidel Castro, Saddam Hussein, or another unprincipled person (in which case, you must change jobs or pay the price of obeying God rather than man), a Christian should do everything possible to give good service to those in authority—and show proper respect. Here are some of Solomon's tips:

1. Begin with a pure heart, which doesn't use manipulation, flattery or force to try to gain concessions.
2. A reasonable attitude, gentle words, and good manners go a long way.
3. Learn to be efficient and good at what you do. Take more courses to better prepare yourself for your job and seek the advice of experts.
4. Don't take advantage of your boss—eating too much of the food provided, sneaking out of work early, or falling down on the job.
5. Don't complain about your supervisors or hang around with those who do.
6. Don't brag or "apple-polish." Your work alone should impress your boss.
7. Patiently pray for changes in your boss. A gentle tongue can "break a bone" a lot faster if it's accompanied by the softening process of *powerful praying*.

☑ Rethinking the Situation

Rob offered Kirk a ride home. "Kirk, how can you always enjoy working so hard?" Rob asked. "And you're nice to everybody, even

Carol. The boss and his wife really think you're hot stuff."

"Anyone can do it," Kirk returned. "It's a matter of following biblical principles. Jesus is our example. He didn't come to be served but to serve. When I think, 'How would Jesus do this job?' or 'How would Jesus treat this person?' it changes the way I work and treat my superiors and co-workers."

"I guess I thought that Christian idealism didn't work in real life," Rob admitted. "On T.V. all I see are strikes and people standing up for their rights."

"I know," replied Kirk, "but find out what God says. He's the ultimate authority, you know." Kirk promised to show him a few Bible verses, and write down some references for him to study and apply. "We Christians march to a different drum beat," Kirk concluded. "Besides, God's principles really work."

 Putting the Truth Into Practice

Reread the seven points taken from Proverbs on page 191. Prayerfully consider a specific way you can implement each guideline and write down what you intend to do about it:

1. _____

_____

2. _____

_____

3. _____

_____

4. _____

_____

5. _____

_____

6. _____

_____

7. _____

Ask the Lord to show you other ways in which you can serve your boss or your teachers, and show personal concern that is not designed to gain something for yourself. Write these things down, and periodically check the list against your actions:

_____

_____

_____

CHAPTER 34

Postscript to a Practical Joke

It was a drab, murky day in March. Exhaust fumes had smudged the once-sparkling white snow into shades of gray and charcoal. Much of it had melted into muddied puddles. As he walked to school, Al felt a gloom on the inside that equaled this dull, late winter day.

When he entered the weathered brick school building, there was more of the same—dingy, off-white walls, and row after row of slate-colored lockers. Classrooms reinforced the same lack-luster theme—blackboards with assignments written on them, open books with black and white pages, gray file cabinets. Even Mr. Niznik wore a white shirt, a black tie, and a salt and pepper wool suit.

If boredom were a fatal disease, Al would be dead. He didn't think he'd survive the rest of the school year, and he longed for something different and exciting—*anything* would do. His mind returned to Mr. Niznik who was again reverting to, "When I began teaching forty years ago . . ." After which he *again* recounted the story of his coming to America as a poor immigrant boy, learning English, getting an education, and now being able to buy a Cadillac. Everyone knew that his new car was the most important thing in Mr. Niznik's life. It was common knowledge that he would never move from Room 111, because it was across from the teacher's parking lot and he wanted to keep an eye on his car at all times.

As he watched the clock, Al determined that he would retire at an early age—while people still looked up to him.

The lunch bell finally rang, and Al, Zane, and Joe headed toward the dreary basement cafeteria. "I'll go crazy," Joe declared, "unless we can do something to lighten up third hour."

"I've got an idea," Zane replied. "We could bring down the house by pulling off an April Fool's special. I could bring my dad's big van to school and park it in a way that would block Mr. Niznik's view of his Cadillac. Al, you arrange to get a counselor's pass so you can distract his attention, while I hide his glasses. Then Joe, you come in tardy and tell him his car is gone. He'll go nuts!"

Because Al was a Christian, he wondered if he should participate in this prank. But he persuaded himself that April Fool's jokes were different, so he went along.

By April first, the snow had disappeared, the sun was out, and everyone had enjoyed a week of spring vacation—but no one dreamed of canceling the prank.

At 11:23 on April 1, Al showed Mr. Niznik his pass for the counselor's office, while Zane snuck up to his cluttered desk to swipe his glasses and his keys. Not being able to find his glasses amid the books and papers on his desk, Mr. Niznik panicked. "Okay," he demanded, "no one goes to lunch until I get my glasses back."

Just then, Joe sauntered in with a tardy pass. "Mr. Niznik," he said, concern in his voice, "Did you park your car where you always do? It's not there! Are you sure you didn't leave your keys in the car?"

Frantically, Mr. Niznik began searching for his keys.

Suddenly, a look of pain crossed his face, and he grabbed for his chair. Moaning in agony, he managed to sit down—and then he slumped over his desk!

▼ ▼ ▼ THIS WAY OUT ▼ ▼ ▼

✔ Asking God to Meet Legitimate Needs

Dear God, you know I like to joke around a lot. Thank you for allowing us to have good, clean fun. Just help me not to go too far. Show me how to place my sense of humor under your control.

✔ Getting the Facts Straight

Like a madman shooting firebrands or deadly arrows is a man who deceives his neighbor and says, "I was only joking!" (Proverbs 26:18–19).

So in everything, do to others what you would have them do to you, for this sums up the Law and the Prophets (Matthew 7:12).

If you're really serious about obeying God, there are some laughs you are going to have to live without. Practical jokes are an American institution—but they're *wrong* if they involve lying, or exposing the other person to treatment you yourself would not like.

Going along with the crowd to tease the kid with the explosive temper, or making "Maladjusted Milly" cry may have become so common that you no longer realize how cruel it is. It's easy to do things without thinking. What if the kid you throw in the pool can't swim, or is wearing an expensive non-waterproof watch? What if your prank call gives Ms. Westfield several sleepless nights? Intentionally leaving Fred at the beach alone with "Miss Misfit" may traumatize them both!

Everybody likes to do crazy, fun things—and God doesn't want you to be straightlaced, somber, and sad. But your teasing and joking *must* stay within the limits of God's Word. When you're uncertain as to whether or not your practical joke will be well received, you'd better stop short. "If in doubt, *don't.*"

✔ Rethinking the Situation

Al couldn't get to sleep. The postscript to their practical joke was a living nightmare. He could never wake up and discover it was just a dream, and he couldn't go to sleep to escape it. Like a video it played over and over in his mind: the school nurse rushing to Mr. Niznik's side and ordering the students out of the room, the medics taking Mr. Niznik out on a stretcher and placing him in an ambulance, the session in the principal's office, and the report that Mr. Niznik had suffered a heart attack and was now fighting for his life.

In the days that followed, Al felt totally condemned. What he'd thought to be a harmless, practical joke had made him a conspirator in a plot that might cost a man's life. He'd already sent a letter of apology to Mrs. Niznik, and had asked God to forgive him at least ten times. But he still felt guilty and he couldn't forgive himself—or get a good night's sleep.

Late one night, he heard a gentle knock on his bedroom door. It was his father.

"I can't sleep either," he began. "Besides, there's something I'd like to share with you." He opened his Bible and read the true story about David committing adultery with Bathsheba—and then he read Psalm 51, David's account of his repentance and receiving the complete forgiveness of God.

"Al," his father began gently, "what David did was worse than your practical joke. But because he believed God and then went on to live like a forgiven man, he continued to be a blessing to many. Forgiveness doesn't depend on how you feel. God says the blood of Jesus, His Son, purifies us from all sin. And He doesn't lie."

Al knew his father was right. He decided to stop listening to Satan's condemnation, to accept God's forgiveness by faith, and to go on with new determination to live for God.

✔ Putting the Truth Into Practice

1. Do you cover up deceit or nasty comments with an I-was-just-kidding reply? God wants honesty instead of alibis because excuses only cover up sin.
2. Have you played some practical jokes you need to apologize for? If so, have you asked God for His forgiveness? Have you made things right with the person you hurt or embarrassed?
3. Rereading this chapter, write out the rules you'll use in the future to decide whether or not you'll participate in a prank:

_____

_____

_____

CHAPTER 35

Revolution in Room 106

It was the first day of school. Looking over her new schedule, Tammy read: "First hour Social Studies, Mr. Sneider." "Oh, no!" she gasped. "It can't be!"

"What's the matter?" Renee asked.

"I have to start every day with Mr. Sneider!" Tammy moaned.

"So do I," Renee comforted. "It's about time we Christians started praying for that man. We believe that God works miracles, and Mr. Sneider is a good place to start. It's not God's will that he spread his atheism and undermine the faith of students."

When the first-hour bell rang, Tammy and Renee had an opportunity to personally size up the teacher about whom they'd heard so much. He seemed eager to draw battle lines. "In this class," he began, "we don't Mickey Mouse around. We face the real issues of life and expose the fiction of traditions. How many of you believe in God?"

Only Renee and Tammy and another girl raised their hands; everyone had been told that in Mr. Sneider's class, atheists got better grades. Immediately Mr. Sneider began to ridicule the girls. He even read from the Bible, making fun of the Ten Commandments.

Very quickly a group of rebels became Mr. Sneider's pets. Each day, they cheered as he attacked authority, made fun of standards of right and wrong, and even passed snide remarks about school discipline policies.

As the days went on, though, it seemed that no one was immune from being belittled by Mr. Sneider—it happened to anyone who disagreed with him on any issue. After a while, even his "pets" became disillusioned. Mr. Sneider had taught at Armstrong High for over twenty years. He was an institution, and because he fought dirty no one dared to take him on.

Renee organized a prayer meeting for Christian students. They prayed for their classmates, their teachers, and their principal. Often they prayed for Mr. Sneider and for God's protection for the Christian students in his classes.

One day, Mr. Sneider began deriding certain school board members and the new principal for establishing stricter rules for teachers and students. He ended with "Renee, don't you agree?" When she didn't, he proceeded to give her some very unbecoming labels, like "phony" and "goody two-shoes."

What Mr. Sneider did not know was that Mr. Vann, the principal, was standing outside the door listening.

A man of courage and conviction, Mr. Vann decided to investigate what was going on. Then he gave Mr. Sneider several specific, written orders. When he refused to comply, they had grounds to fire him for insubordination.

When students received the news that Mr. Sneider had been let go, they were elated. Some kids even threw a party to celebrate. "Mr. Sneider would be shocked to realize how powerful prayer really is," Renee remarked. "Who should we start praying for next?"

▼ ▼ ▼ THIS WAY OUT ▼ ▼ ▼

☑ Asking God to Meet Legitimate Needs

Dear God, I know you hate injustice and desire that good win out. I pray that you'll remove the wicked authorities and replace

them with people who are fair and just. Also help me to be honest
and efficient in any place of responsibility that I fill.

☑ Getting the Facts Straight

When the righteous triumph, there is great elation; but when
the wicked rise to power, men go into hiding (Proverbs 28:12).

When the righteous thrive, the people rejoice; when the
wicked rule, the people groan (Proverbs 29:2).

When the righteous prosper, the city rejoices; when the
wicked perish, there are shouts of joy. Through the blessing of
the upright a city is exalted, but by the mouth of the wicked it is
destroyed (Proverbs 11:10–11).

When the wicked rise to power, people go into hiding; but
when the wicked perish, the righteous thrive (Proverbs 28:28).

If bad rulers govern, sin is not punished and those who live for
Jesus are persecuted. Christians are to respect authority, and *not*
overthrow it by force. Yet we have at our disposal the greatest power
in the world—and that power is *prayer.* By praying for those in authority over us and asking God to remove the unjust, Christians can
greatly influence their country, their neighborhoods, and the environment at work or school. Be a prayer warrior who spreads happiness
by praying for those in leadership positions.

Remember too that you can be a cause of joy if you act uprightly
in all you do. Maybe you don't have much influence yet, but start
practicing integrity and excellence in all you do. Be the best head of
the clean-up committee, keep good track of the money brought in
from the car wash, or plan a super meeting for the youth group.
Someday, many may rejoice because of your righteous leadership.

☑ Rethinking the Situation

Monday morning, everybody peeked into Room 106 to get a look
at the new teacher, Mr. Baker. He was a clean-cut blond with an
athletic build, and he'd just graduated from college. He was getting
the class off to a pleasant start when Butch rudely interrupted to ask
if he believed in God. "Yes," he said, smiling, "I've accepted Jesus
Christ as my Savior, and it's the greatest thing that ever happened to
me." Renee and Tammy couldn't hide their joy.

"Well, I'm an atheist," Butch shot back. "Only ignorant people believe in God."

Unruffled, Mr. Baker replied, "You have a right to your opinion. I personally have a hard time believing that we all got here by chance."

Realizing that Mr. Baker respected each student, a lot of kids stopped being intimidated, and their class discussions became really interesting. Soon it was evident there were three other Christian students in the class! Most kids were interested in hearing Christian viewpoints on many subjects. It was incredible how having a righteous man in authority had changed the atmosphere completely.

The prayer group became more enthusiastic about praying for their teachers and principal. Several students accepted Christ, and the principal was very impressed by the Christians on campus. At the end of the year, Miss Steward, the English teacher, gave her life to Jesus. Many victories resulted from the same prayer meeting that caused the revolution in Room 106.

✔ Putting the Truth Into Practice

List the authorities in your life: parents, pastors, teachers, coaches, bosses, government officials (such as mayor, governor, President). Decide to pray for all of them daily, if possible, but at least once a week.

Also list the situations in which you're placed in authority: baby-sitting, supervising people at work, teaching Sunday school, monitoring younger brothers and sisters, nieces and nephews. Pray for the children you baby-sit, the people you're in charge of at work, and the younger children you influence.

Learning to be under authority, and praying for those over you, will help you be the kind of authority God wants you to be. Someday you may be the coach, teacher, or boss you're now praying for. Ask God to make you a blessing to those who are under you right now.

CHAPTER 36

The Cure for "I-itis"

If there's one thing Dorian had been taught since he could walk, it was to stick up for his rights. His mother was a leader in the Woman's Liberation Movement, secretary of the local chapter of Keep America Green, and a member of the American Civil Liberties Union. If he complained of unfair treatment at school, his mother was always ready to go to bat for him. Watchdog for her son's freedom, she was a leader in P.T.A., Little League Mothers—any group in which she could use her influence to protect her son.

Dorian didn't have to wear his "Don't Push Me Around" T-shirt for people to notice his existence. He was the first to complain about the soggy French fries and demand his money back. He let his teachers know when he was dissatisfied with the class or the grading system. Taking the best seat, butting into line, or demanding all the attention didn't bother him in the least. After all, it was "the survival of the fittest," and he was determined to be on top.

His mother had promised him a party for making National Honor Society. Since he had a 3.81 average, he was sure he was in. He had nice invitations printed and had already passed out a couple before the names were announced over the loudspeaker in homeroom. He was never mentioned.

Angry, he marched down to the office and bawled out the secretary for not typing the list correctly. Overhearing the scene, the principal came out of his office.

"Dorian, you're a *pain*. National Honor Society members must demonstrate service, leadership, and character as well as scholarship. You demand to be treated like a king, and you bully everybody. I have the list, and not one teacher voted for you."

The only way Dorian knew to compensate for his losses was to become more aggressive. Since he'd just turned eighteen, he went to see a lawyer and they drew up a suit, contending that electing students to the National Honor Society by non-objective means was discriminatory.

Although Dorian's family spent a lot of money on the case, they lost not only in court, but also in school. Students had disliked Dorian before—now most kids hated him.

Marla was one of the few who paid any attention to him. Dorian decided to use the only techniques he knew to win her affection. He bragged about his plans to become a lawyer, showed her pictures of his luxurious home, and one day after school invited her to the fanciest restaurant in town. But Marla said she had a date with Tom. Dorian couldn't believe it. He thought of Tom as a Milquetoast—sickeningly polite, much too quiet, overly responsible, and one who always let other people run all over him.

"Marla," he couldn't resist asking, "what do you *see* in Tom?"

"He's a perfect gentleman," Marla replied. "He relies on the power of Jesus, and he knows how to love his enemies. He puts the interests of others above his own. He's a great guy." For once Dorian had nothing to say.

Marla continued: "Tom and I are praying for you. When you don't have God to protect you, life can be pretty tough. Not possessing God's dynamite power to love and forgive only results in bitterness and frustration. Your life could be different, Dorian. . . ."

▼ ▼ ▼ THIS WAY OUT ▼ ▼ ▼

✔ Asking God to Meet Legitimate Needs

Dear God, right now I feel like everyone's bossing me around and criticizing me. It would really be nice to hear some compliments. Keep me from becoming rebellious. Lord, I ask you for your protection. Thank you that you love me and think I'm great. Please place someone in my life who has the gift of building up people like me.

✔ Getting the Facts Straight

Do not exalt yourself in the king's presence, and do not claim a place among great men; it is better for him to say to you, "Come up here," than for him to humiliate you before a nobleman. What you have seen with your eyes do not bring hastily to court, for what will you do in the end if your neighbor puts you to shame? (Proverbs 25:6–8).

Let another praise you, and not your own mouth; someone else, and not your own lips (Proverbs 27:2).

Honor one another above yourselves (Romans 12:10).

The pushy person who personifies self-advancement doesn't make a good friend, a good neighbor, or a good citizen. But it's important to see why so many people are bummed-out on being good. Those who haven't plugged into God's supernatural power (and Christians who haven't turned on the switch!) will feel like constant losers in the struggle with selfishness.

All our learning about good manners and observing "the golden rule" will vanish when the stakes are high enough, if we rely only on self-effort. We say, "Every man has his price." Not taking God into consideration, proponents of many modern ideologies say, "Why put on a front? It's more sensible to proclaim that self-interest is right and to stop making people feel guilty about looking out for 'number one.' "

Only love that comes from Jesus gives us the will to genuinely want to put others above ourselves. Only the security of knowing that an all-powerful God is protecting us makes it unnecessary to defend our every statement, or to constantly stand guard so that no one takes advantage of us. Only knowing that God considers us so valuable that He sent His Son to die for us can remove the temptation to tell everyone how great we are. There's all the difference in the world between proposing "Pollyanna platitudes" and letting Jesus live His selfless life of love and compassion through you.

🗸 Rethinking the Situation

Just then Tom came along. "I was just explaining to Dorian how knowing Jesus personally can change his whole outlook on life," Marla told him.

"That's great!" Tom exclaimed. "I've got my mom's car. Let's go to McDonalds and talk about it some more." Marla climbed into the backseat so Dorian wouldn't feel left out, and so that he could talk more with Tom.

Although Marla and Tom ordered only Cokes and Dorian asked for two double cheeseburgers and a shake, Tom picked up the check. Dorian was impressed by the fact that they really cared about him.

"My mom's an atheist," Dorian informed them. "I've never been inside a church and I've never opened a Bible."

"We're praying for you, Dorian," Tom began, "because we know that you've never had the opportunity to learn what *real* Christianity is.

"But you've probably noticed," Tom continued, "that your philosophy of life alienates you from people and makes you miserable. That's because going against God's design for the way we're supposed to treat each other produces unpleasant consequences. Resentment, anger, and worry can cause physical symptoms, like ulcers and high blood pressure. Hate can even make a beautiful girl ugly."

"I can see your point," Dorian conceded. "I admire Marla because she's so kind and so genuine. I just asked her out, but she said she had a date with you. You're unbelievable—here I am, a potential rival, and you're buying me food. You're concerned about my happiness. I need whatever it is you two have inside."

Tom explained the Gospel to Dorian, and he accepted Christ.

In the months to come, as he grew in his faith, Dorian let God be his lawyer. He found great joy in putting the needs of others above his own. He discovered the cure for "I-itis."

🗸 Putting the Truth Into Practice

Which of the following would be the biggest temptations for you?

_____ To tell the whole world you got an A on the biology final.

_____ To not give up until you prove you're right to anyone who doubts you.

_____ To take the most comfortable seat first, before the room fills up for the Tuesday night Bible study.

_____ To become offended if the pastor doesn't choose you as one of the youth group leaders.

_____ To interrupt the teacher's praise of John for working so hard at the car wash to inform her that you put in more hours than he did.

_____ To give a couple of hints so people will ask you about the vocal contest you just won.

_____ To quickly affirm that the misunderstanding was all Connie's fault.

_____ To explain how nervous you were and how badly you played at the recital so someone will rave about your piano playing.

_____ To butt into the lunch line.

Reread the scripture verses given in "Getting the Facts Straight." Memorize the verse that applies to your temptation, and rely on the power of Jesus to put it into practice.

Self—Examination

Part IV: The Fine Art of Getting Along With People

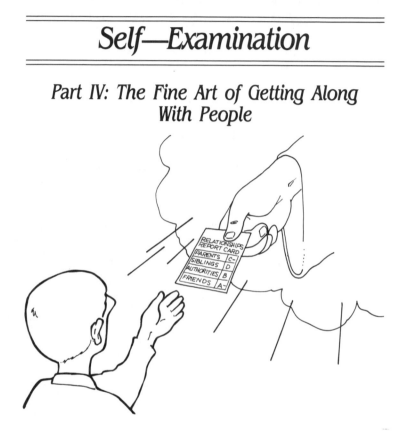

Fill in the blank with the correct scrambled word (listed on the next page).

1. The king's heart is in the hand of the_____ .
2. It is the Lord's _____ that prevails.
3. The Devil is a master _____ .
4. Do not despise your _____ when she is old.
5. A man of knowledge uses words with _____ .
6. It is his glory to overlook an _____ .
7. He who covers an offense promotes _____ .

8. A _____ man will be richly blessed.
9. Learn to thank God for _____ .
10. Evil comes to him who _____ for it.
11. The _____ of your decisions will determine the course of your life.
12. Finding out where the other person is coming from always requires more _____ than speaking.
13. Learning to please your _____ and your boss is extremely important.
14. Your _____ and joking must stay within the limits of God's Word.
15. If in _____ , don't.
16. When the righteous thrive, people _____ .
17. When the wicked perish there are _____ of joy.
18. Do not _____ yourself in the king's presence.
19. Honor one another above _____ .

HSEESCAR	STINAGE	FFSEENO
GTYENHREVI	DLRO	TSUHOS
ERCEOJI	LTFFUHAI	CQNNCEEEUSSO
RMHOTE	SREEVLYSOU	TDUBO
VLEO	TTRRENSAI	XATLE
GLININETS	STEAHCRE	EPOPURS
VEERIEDC		

16. rejoice. 17. shouts. 18. exalt. 19. yourselves.
11. consequences. 12. listening. 13. teachers. 14. teasing. 15. doubt.
6. offense. 7. love. 8. faithful. 9. everything. 10. searches.
ANSWERS: 1. Lord. 2. purpose. 3. deceiver. 4. mother. 5. restraint.

Part Five

Tips for Teens—Variety Pack

CHAPTER 37

Desire's Devastating Detour

Alina was a dreamer. She loved beautiful things, and as a result she had big problems living within her budget.

Having grown up on the coast, she and the sea had something special going. Sailing was a passion, and Alina also enjoyed swimming, surfing, and snorkeling. Her fantasies always included a guy rich enough to build her the dream home she was already designing, and buy her a yacht. She wanted a husband who loved the ocean as much as she did.

When she and Susie headed for the beach one sunny August afternoon, Alina didn't know that this day would change her life for a long time.

She didn't know his name then, but there was a certain well-built, sunburned, blond surfer she just couldn't get out of her mind. And after she learned his name was Drake, he began to fill the role of prince charming in her daydreams.

When school started, she was delighted to discover that Drake was in her English class. Not only that, but alphabetical seating placed him across the aisle from her. Alina paid special attention to her appearance, and made sure that she smiled a lot. Soon she and Drake were talking to each other nearly every day before class began. She learned that he had won several surfing awards and that his family owned a yacht! The man of her dreams had appeared on the scene.

But soon Alina's ecstasy changed to frustration. Drake was pleasant and talkative before class, but he'd pass her in the hall without even saying "hello." Then Alina learned that he was dating Carla. Seeing them together during lunch became pure torture. She began to feel jealous. It was evident from the clothes Carla wore that her parents had a lot of money. Alina began to feel inferior and shabby.

When Drake and Carla broke up, Alina thought she'd have a chance. Although Drake was friendly enough in English class, he never showed any special interest in Alina. The more she found out about Drake, the better he fit her dream dimensions. Unable to do anything more to attract his attention, Alina became more and more desperate, a prisoner of the fantasy she herself had invented.

◆ ◆ ◆ THIS WAY OUT ◆ ◆ ◆

☞ Asking God to Meet Legitimate Needs

God gave you the ability to dream and to plan for the future. Creativity is a gift from Him, and He wants you to use it. We're born with the capacity to set up lofty goals and to make big plans for the future. But our aspirations must fit within the framework of biblical principles, and our wills must be surrendered to God—or the very dreams we cherish become our prison. It is essential that you constantly submit your goals to God and let Him make the necessary changes. Wayward wishes and uncontrolled longings have ruined many lives.

> *Dear God, my desires are giving me problems again. I want _____ and _____ right now! I give these dreams to you. Give me what is best in your time.*

☛ Getting the Facts Straight

> Hope deferred makes the heart sick, but a longing fulfilled is a tree of life (Proverbs 13:12).

> A longing fulfilled is sweet to the soul, but fools detest turning from evil (Proverbs 13:19).

> Do not let your heart envy sinners, but always be zealous for the fear of the Lord. There is surely a future hope for you, and your hope will not be cut off (Proverbs 23:17–18).

> Know also that wisdom is sweet to your soul; if you find it, there is a future hope for you, and your hope will not be cut off (Proverbs 24:14).

Your desires and hopes are very important in shaping your destiny. The Devil knows this, so he tries to get you to set your heart on actions that involve disobedience, or on something that can't be proven scripturally to be God's will for your life. Once you've decided you can't live without Darren or Darla or a Harley Davidson, or that dress in the window at Nordstroms, or an A in chemistry, the Devil can give you some heavy duty temptation. He may tell you that the only way to keep your heartthrob is by lowering your moral standards. Cheating or shoplifting or working thirty hours a week, plus going to school, may be the only way you can attain the goal you won't release to God. The Devil can easily push you over the edge.

As an "answer," Eastern religions try to wipe out human desire completely. Becoming a zombie does help you eliminate the pain of unfulfilled longing, but it also makes you miss the joy of exercising God-given creativity, planning for the future, and seeing dreams realized.

God has a better way. If you submit every desire to Him, He will judge its worth according to His infinite wisdom. Obviously, living with a real respect for God and His Word already knocks out a lot of destructive goals, such as dishonest gain, marrying a non-Christian, and living in luxury and indulgence. If you take a not-my-will-but-yours-be-done attitude, and submit your dreams to God (who loves you unconditionally and knows what's best for you), the sad tale of following a wrong desire to the brink of disaster will not be the story of your life.

By wanting to follow Jesus more than anything else, and always being willing to give up your comforts, conveniences, and future plans to Him, you'll save yourself a lot of frustration. Clinging to misplaced hope is a recipe for disaster.

☞ Rethinking the Situation

Unable to stand it any longer (but not courageous enough to go right up and ask Drake how he felt about her), Alina decided to write him a letter. She spent days composing it—and she told him everything: how she had liked him the moment she saw him on the beach, her dream of meeting someone who enjoyed all the things she loved so much, and her desire to date him. She asked if he ever had similar feelings toward her.

What she didn't know was that Skip had a score to settle with Drake. When he saw Alina carefully slip Drake a sealed envelope in English class, he snatched it away. "Teacher's intuition" brought Mr. Bauer immediately to the scene of the commotion, and the three students meekly returned to writing impromptu themes.

But the next morning, Skip was standing outside school with xeroxed copies of Alina's letter! "*Extra!* Extra! The secret love of Alina and Drake—read all about it!"

Alina, who always entered by the side door, arrived at her locker still worried about the fate of her letter. Just then Susie approached her with a copy of the letter. "Did you *write* this?" she asked.

Alina turned white, and Susie thought she was going to faint. When Alina recovered enough to ask where she'd gotten the letter, Susie told her the mortifying truth. She was so angry and upset that it was all she could do to make her way to the nurse's office and get herself sent home "sick."

Alone in her room, Alina felt miserable. She vowed never to tell her parents what had happened: They just wouldn't understand—besides, they were too busy running their own lives to take much interest in her problems. Alina was so humiliated and depressed she even thought of suicide.

At 3:30 the doorbell rang. It was Susie. Although she'd warned Alina many times about feeding the unscriptural desire to date a non-Christian, Susie didn't say, "I told you so."

Instead, she asked a penetrating question: "Alina, I know you prayed and asked Jesus into your life a year ago, but did you really understand what you were doing?"

"I guess so," Alina replied. "Why do you ask?"

"Because it seems so hard for you to understand that Jesus has the right to run your life," Susie explained. "I wondered if you only repeated some words, without opening the door of your heart and giving yourself completely to the Lord. Who's your first love—Jesus or Drake? Does Jesus really live inside you?"

"When you put it that way, I guess I'd have to say *no*," Alina admitted.

Susie used some scriptures to show Alina that when Jesus enters a heart He comes in to take over. Then she summed it up: "Either He's Lord *of all*, or He's not Lord *at all*." At last, Alina understood what being a Christian was all about. She surrendered her life to Jesus.

In spite of everything, she experienced a peace deep down inside. And now she realized that God gives us biblical rules because He loves us and wants to protect us. Now she could see that she had to submit her dreams to Jesus for His approval.

Susie concluded saying, "This is probably the best thing that could have happened to you. Drake is not a Christian or a good influence. God may have used Skip to save you from straying away from Him, from sex before marriage, from a dependent relationship, or even from following your dream into a miserable marriage."

Although her heart ached—and she was embarrassed to face the kids at school—Alina had to agree with Susie.

☑ Putting the Truth Into Practice

Include all your dreams in the chart on the next page. After filling in all the blanks, pray daily, asking God to change the goals that are not in line with His will.

DREAM	POSSIBLE PITFALLS	SCRIPTURE(S) THAT APPLIES
To marry a very beautiful girl, or an extremely handsome guy.	I could make a bad choice, because I'm too concerned with physical appearance.	"The Lord does not look at the things man looks at. Man looks at the outward appearance but the Lord looks at the heart" (1 Samuel 16:7). "Charm is deceptive, and beauty is fleeting; but a woman who fears the Lord is to be praised" (Proverbs 31:30).

CHAPTER 38

The Gift of a Happy Heart

Jillian lived with her mother and grandmother, and was told that her father had died shortly after her mother became pregnant—but before they could be married. She wondered if the story was true.

There was no doubt her mother and grandmother had lived tough lives—or that hers would be equally hard. In her home, self-pity was queen. The conversation revolved around complaints of unfair treatment, past wrongs and present problems. Jillian absorbed that pessimistic outlook on life. She didn't like school, and thought the teachers were out to get her. She resented the fact that she didn't receive any attention from guys, and blamed God for creating her ugly. She was jealous of girls who had fathers and brothers and sisters. With so many strikes against her, she felt she was doomed to failure.

When Jillian was ten she had attended a week of Vacation Bible School, and at that time she had accepted Christ as her Savior. Since the church was only two blocks from her house and the people were nice to her, she continued to attend. Although she loved Jesus, she didn't really experience the joy of her salvation.

As she grew older, the kids in the youth group tolerated her, but no one wanted to listen to her tales of woe. More and more, Jillian began to give up on life. She felt caught in a vicious circle of migraine headaches, loneliness and "bad breaks." She assumed that no one in her situation could ever be happy.

But that was before Pam moved into her neighborhood and started attending Jillian's church. The first thing anyone noticed about Pam was a terrible scar on her face. Closer observation revealed that she had an artificial leg and walked with difficulty. But her smile and resilience were disarming. She entered into activities with enthusiasm, and was even a good volleyball player! She soon had a lot of friends.

One night at youth fellowship, the Pastor asked Pam to play the piano and give her testimony. She was a fantastic pianist, and the way she played gospel songs made a big impact. Then she rose to tell her story:

When she was seven years old, an automobile accident killed her parents, her two brothers and one sister, and it left her handicapped. As she relived adjusting to the loss of her family and learning to walk again, tears filled the eyes of many in the room. Now she lived with her grandparents, and explained that she wasn't able to participate in all the activities because her grandmother's health was poor and she had to do most of the housework. She summed it up by saying, "My life has not been easy, but I know God has a purpose for everything. He's used me to help other kids who feel that life has cheated them in some way. God *is* faithful. Each problem is an opportunity to draw closer to Him and experience His provision for every need."

Jillian couldn't believe what she was hearing. Pam wasn't a fake. *Could it be that my ideas about life are wrong?* she wondered. *Have I put my own limits on God?*

▼ ▼ ▼ THIS WAY OUT ▼ ▼ ▼

☑ Asking God to Meet Legitimate Needs

Dear God, I know I can't depend on my circumstances for happiness, and that true joy comes from you. Your Word tells me,

"The joy of the Lord is your strength" (Nehemiah 8:10). Right now
_____ *and* _____ *are making me sad.*
I'm leaving these problems in your hands. Give me your joy and
peace for this day.

☑ Getting the Facts Straight

A happy heart makes the face cheerful, but heartache crushes
the spirit (Proverbs 15:13).

All the days of the oppressed are wretched, but the cheerful
heart has a continual feast (Proverbs 15:15).

A cheerful look brings joy to the heart, and good news gives
health to the bones (Proverbs 15:30).

A cheerful heart is good medicine, but a crushed spirit dries
up the bones (Proverbs 17:22).

A man's spirit sustains him in sickness, but a crushed spirit
who can bear? (Proverbs 18:14).

You probably don't need to be convinced that a cheerful heart is a
great asset. A contented person can overcome great problems, maintain better health, and constantly inspire others. The big question is,
Where do happy hearts come from?

When Jesus was praying for His disciples, He said, "I say these
things while I am still in the world, so that they may have the full
measure of my joy within them" (John 17:13). By accepting the promises Jesus has given us, we can receive all His joy. Steadfastly believing
everything He has said can dispel sadness.

Even at a graveside these words give hope: "He will wipe every
tear from their eyes. There will be no more death or mourning or
crying or pain, for the old order of things has passed away. He who
was seated on the throne said, 'I am making everything new' " (Rev-
elations 21:4–5). When your heart aches and you ask the question
why? you can still rejoice in this truth: "In him we were also chosen,
having been predestined according to the plan of him who works out
everything in conformity with the purpose of his will" (Ephesians
1:11). If it seems like everything is against you, claim Jeremiah 29:11:
" 'For I know the plans I have for you,' declares the Lord, 'plans to
prosper you and not to harm you, plans to give you hope and a future.' "

Do you *really* believe that God knows what He's doing and that He has your best interests in mind? As a child, I contracted a rare mouth disease. When my parents put the medicine on my raw gums, the pain was excruciating. My sister learned to run out of earshot before I began to scream. In spite of the ordeal, I trusted my parents and knew they were trying to help me. I was too little to understand how the medicine worked. I only knew that my parents always acted for my good. Put that kind of faith in God, and then not even the most ugly of circumstances can turn off your joy.

Form the habit of constantly praising God and giving thanks in all things. When you face overwhelming problems, thank God that He's in control and that He will work out everything for your benefit. Praise God for the rain and for the storm. A grateful heart is a happy heart.

The Devil is capable of dropping a cloud of depression on you. *Don't accept it.* Nearly everyone has noticed that there is a clever satanic strategy that sends several kinds of difficulties your way at once. The enemy wants you to lose your joy so he can torture you. Just remember that the God who can solve one problem at a time is capable of getting you out of the six impossible situations you're facing all at once. Learn to stand on God's promises instead of falling for feelings of hopelessness and despair.

◢ Rethinking the Situation

After the youth meeting, Jillian approached Pam. "How do you do it?" she asked. "I've been feeling sorry for myself ever since I can remember."

"Let's get some cake and hot chocolate before we sit down," Pam suggested.

When they'd found a secluded place to sit, Pam smiled and began. "I don't do it, God does. When I was in the hospital recuperating from the accident, it was hard to adjust to the loss of my family. My grandmother visited me every day, and told me, 'God loves you very much and has a special purpose for what has happened. He's ready to make your life into a miracle—if you'll only let Him.'

"First, they said I'd never walk again, but we prayed and prayed. It took a long time, but I even learned to run. And I thought I couldn't live without my family, but I ask Jesus every day to fill the loneliness in my heart—and He keeps sending me Christian brothers and sisters and mothers and fathers. God even provided for me to take piano lessons with the best teacher in the city. Now my counselor says I may be in line for a full-tuition music scholarship. His blessings never end.

"Jillian," Pam asked, "are you mad at God about something?"

"Yes," Jillian admitted. "I blame Him for allowing me to be born illegitimate, for creating me ugly, and for not giving me a fair chance."

"Confess all that to Him," Pam urged, "and then practice thanking Him and praising Him for every little thing. I thank Him for my almost-good leg, for sunshine, for homework, for a chance to learn to be a good cook, for ice cream cones—for everything!"

Jillian did ask forgiveness for blaming God, and for her unwillingness to trust Him to turn evil into good. Little by little she learned to be thankful and to really trust God for a loving plan that was bigger than her understanding. She began smiling more, working harder, and experiencing fewer headaches.

Stopping by the card shop before Valentine's Day, she noticed the advertisement for giant heart-shaped cards that featured faces and smiles: "Give the gift of a happy heart." She chuckled to herself. Now she knew that God was the only one who could really do that.

✔ Putting the Truth Into Practice

1. List the things for which you've blamed God.
2. List the reasons you're bitter toward others.
3. Confess the sin of holding a grudge against God or other people. Ask God to remove your resentment..
4. After each item write out these verses:

> I am the Lord, the God of all mankind. Is anything too hard for me? (Jeremiah 32:27)
>
> I have loved you with an everlasting love: I have drawn you with loving-kindness. I will build you up again and you will be rebuilt (Jeremiah 31:3–4).
>
> He has sent me to bind up the brokenhearted, to proclaim freedom for the captives and release from darkness for the captives . . . to comfort all who mourn . . . to bestow on them a crown of beauty instead of ashes, the oil of gladness instead of mourning, and a garment of praise instead of a spirit of despair (Isaiah 61:1–3).

> Make the message of each of these verses yours, and it will change each wrong attitude you've acquired.

CHAPTER 39

Face Value vs. True Worth

Bob and Barbie were twins. When they moved from Chicago to a small town in Wisconsin, they found that the forty-four students in the junior class, most of whom had known each other since grade school, were bored with seeing the same people, following the same routine and going to the same places. The newcomers from the big city were showered with attention—and became instant celebrities.

Bob couldn't help but notice that Brooke, a strikingly gorgeous brunette, gave him special attention. He felt flattered. Because he was so shy, he didn't have much experience with girls. He'd also been taught never to date a non-Christian, but Brooke's incredible beauty lowered his resistance. She asked him for a ride to work, borrowed money from him, and even begged for the answers to the history assignment.

When the Valentine's Sweetheart Banquet was announced, Brooke invited him and he accepted. That night, for the first time, he saw how loud and obnoxious she really was. She flirted with other guys, and gossiped constantly. When she started conning him to get up at 6:00 the next morning to drive her to the city sixty miles away, Bob wasn't quite sure how to say no.

Consequently, he ended up being her chauffeur. But when she asked to borrow $50 to go shopping, he'd had enough of Brooke.

Bob and Barbie were very close and usually talked things over—but that was before their sudden popularity. Careful to obey her parents and to avoid close friendships with non-Christians, Barbie had never had a real date in her whole life.

While Bob was being chased by Brooke, Barbie was also drawing attention. When Clark, who was strikingly handsome, super intelligent, and the son of the richest man in town, asked her if she wanted a ride in his sports car, she never even thought of saying no.

The next day he sent her a dozen roses. She was overwhelmed. At first she didn't notice that he constantly talked about himself, acted superior, or that he threw his money around to impress everyone.

One day when Clark went to great lengths to prove the chemistry teacher wrong, Barbie felt a little uncomfortable, but she still admired his brains. The vulgar remark he made when Dean didn't know the name of the sixteenth President disturbed her a lot. When her turn came to be put down, she cried.

But being invited out to something like the Sweetheart Banquet by a handsome guy had been her dream for a long time. She accepted his invitation—against her better judgment.

Clark gave her a gorgeous white orchid corsage and brought the whole family chocolates. And that was the end of his chivalry. It didn't take Barbie long to realize that staying home with a book would have been more pleasant than attending the Sweetheart Banquet with Clark. No matter what topic was brought up, he rudely interrupted to tell all he knew about it. When Barbie tried to explain the plot of a book he hadn't read, he invented an ending and said he really enjoyed the novel. Just to show off, he thoroughly humiliated the waitress. Barbie decided then and there never to go out with him again.

Barbie was just getting up when Bob returned from the city. Their mother had prepared a special breakfast and their father informed them that he wanted to have a serious talk.

♥ ♥ ♥ THIS WAY OUT ♥ ♥ ♥

🗹 Asking God to Meet Legitimate Needs

Dear God, I know that "man looks at the outward appearance, but the Lord looks at the heart." Teach me to judge people the way you do. Help me not to be fooled by good looks, nice clothes, or a pleasing personality. Give me your wisdom in choosing my friends.

🗹 Getting the Facts Straight

Like a gold ring in a pig's snout is a beautiful woman who shows no discretion (Proverbs 11:22).

Your beauty should not come from outward adornment, such as braided hair and the wearing of gold jewelry and fine clothes. Instead, it should be that of your inner self, the unfading beauty of a gentle and quiet spirit, which is of great worth in God's sight (1 Peter 3:3–4).

A prudent man keeps his knowledge to himself, but the heart of fools blurts out folly (Proverbs 12:23).

But the wisdom that comes from heaven is first of all pure; then peace-loving, considerate, submissive, full of mercy and good fruit, impartial and sincere (James 3:17).

You are conditioned by your culture to respect good looks, brains, and success. And it's fine to look your best, to study hard, and to put your heart into whatever you attempt. Remembering that your body is the temple of the Holy Spirit should cause you to dress both modestly and attractively. Learning all you can and undertaking each project with enthusiasm is part of glorifying God in all we do.

But the things God prizes most—and we should adopt the standards of our Father—are a gentle spirit, purity, submissiveness, mercy, goodness, sincerity, consideration of others, a heart for God, and an ability to spread peace.

First of all, this concept should comfort you: You can be great even if you're not especially good-looking, terribly successful, or super intelligent. All you need to do is to allow the Holy Spirit to place His fruit—love, joy, peace, patience, kindness, goodness, faithfulness, gentleness, and self-control—in your life.

Secondly, it should make you examine how you live. How much time do you spend at Jesus' feet learning humility and love? How much of God's Word do you hide in your heart? Are you determined to cultivate the qualities He displayed? Or are you caught up in dressing "just right," being "cool," and proving yourself to be successful?

Finally, you should use God's yardstick in choosing your friends. Look for the hidden treasure of a quiet spirit and a heart of wisdom, rather than a fantastic figure, an athletic build, a brilliant mind, or the splash of success.

🢒 Rethinking the Situation

After they sat down at the breakfast table and said grace, the twins' mom served blueberry pancakes. Their father cleared his throat and broke the suspense. "We're worried about you kids," he began. "We're afraid that you've made some friends who are bad influences."

"We know that part of it is our fault for not keeping closer tabs on you," their mother apologized. "Your father had to work overtime to set up the office here, and I was so busy unpacking and getting the house in order that I think we neglected you. And in an entirely new environment, it's easier to make some errors in judgment.

"Last night after you left for the Valentine's Banquet," she continued, "I had a visit from the lady across the street. She told me that Brooke has had two abortions, and that she wouldn't let any son of hers go near the girl. She also informed me that Clark's folks are into astrology. I realize it's possible she could be wrong, but we do need to be careful who we associate with. We already know that there's no Bible-believing church in this town. And even though things seem a lot tamer than Chicago, we still must be wise in our choice of friends."

"Mom, you don't have to worry," Bob comforted. "Last night I realized how selfish Brooke really is. I've already told her to find someone else. I know now how easy it is for a beautiful girl to con a guy."

"I used to think that the way Christians always talk about *inner qualities* was pretty stuffy," Barbie put in. "But now I can see how shallow people are if Jesus doesn't live in them. I know that most non-believers have better manners than Clark, but believe me, I won't even think of dating a non-Christian again."

"Because we'll have to drive thirty miles to attend a good church, finding Christian friends won't be easy here. You'll sometimes feel left out. But following Jesus is always worth it," their father counseled.

"I know," Barbie agreed. "We can witness to the kids here and those who accept Christ can be our friends."

✔ Putting the Truth Into Practice

HOMEWORK FOR THE "SCHOOL OF INNER BEAUTY"

1. Practice gentleness in the way you answer your parents, sisters and brothers.
2. Exercise a quiet spirit when things don't go your way, or you're forced to do something you dislike.
3. Plan to read and see only those things that will help keep your mind pure.
4. Learn to be a peacemaker in family squabbles.
5. When there's not enough food to go around, or when not everyone fits into the first carload bound for the beach, practice thinking of others before yourself.
6. Exercise a submissive attitude, even when a parent or a teacher is being unreasonable.
7. When someone wrongs you, look upon that person with an attitude of mercy and a willingness to forgive.
8. Allow the Holy Spirit to manifest His fruit in you—love, joy, peace, patience, kindness, goodness, faithfulness, gentleness, and self-control.
9. Avoid showing off, or scheming to deceive others.

CHAPTER 40

The Spoke That Tried to Replace the Wheel

No one could accuse Krista of a lack of initiative. She was definitely a go-for-it girl. She did tend to go overboard, however.

When she decided to become the best-dressed girl in Lakeview High, she not only worked twenty hours a week to supplement her large allowance, she read fashion magazines, went to style shows, and took a modeling course. She spent hours shopping for accessories, and her mirror became her best friend. Her hairdo, make-up, and outfit had to be perfect.

But that was before she got to know Brett. Handsome, warm, and intelligent, he was decidedly casual.

After waiting an hour for Krista to change clothes and primp (just to stop by Burger King), Brett explained his philosophy of life—avoid stress, dress comfortably, be yourself, and don't try to impress anyone. Because she was crazy about him, she decided to do everything possible to fit into his mold. Sweatshirts, T-shirts, and blue jeans began to replace her designer clothes. At times she almost appeared sloppy. Brett became her obsession—there was nothing she wouldn't do to please him.

But when their relationship ended, she was brokenhearted. And although she didn't feel like it, she decided to find another "goal." She'd gained some weight, and didn't want to build another wardrobe from scratch—besides, she'd come to enjoy the freedom of dressing casually. Because Krista had had swimming lessons since age four, it was easy to decide to put all her energies into being a champion for the swim team. She began to live at the pool. Hours and hours of work perfected her dives. She made it to state competition—and the coach even talked of her going to the Olympics!

The night before the state meet, Krista didn't feel well but thought it was just nerves. Then the next morning she awoke with chills, fever, and stomach cramps. She began vomiting and became so weak she could barely raise her head above the pillow. Having lost her chance to win state, she was confined to bed for a week.

Her illness forced her to think about her direction in life. She'd put her heart into many different things without receiving inner satisfaction. That night she had a dream. She dreamed that Jesus came to visit her home. While they were having a Coke, Jesus said to her, "Krista, if you put me first in your life, everything else will fall into its proper place."

▼ ▼ ▼ THIS WAY OUT ▼ ▼ ▼

☑ Asking God to Meet Legitimate Needs

Dear God, help me to put you first in everything. I know that if I do, you'll show me how to put balance into my life. Right now _____ is an area that I'm neglecting. _____ seems to be the spoke that's too long for the wheel. Give me your wisdom to take the steps I need to remedy the situation.

☑ Getting the Facts Straight

If you find honey, eat just enough—too much of it, and you will vomit (Proverbs 25:16).

But seek first his kingdom and his righteousness, and all these things will be given to you as well (Matthew 6:33).

We're all too good at going to extremes—crash diets, four-hour-a-day physical fitness programs, buying the most expensive ski equipment and planning to go to the slopes five days a week, or spending an inordinate amount of time and money to have exactly the "right" clothes. God has the formula for a balanced life: Seek first the kingdom of God.

Obviously, the most important person in the kingdom is the King. Utmost attention must be given to loving Him, adoring Him and obeying Him. If looking for God and His righteousness is your number-one priority, other things *will* fall in line.

It is important to see that God, not what we can do for Him, should be our first priority. For instance, some people spend so much time witnessing that they don't take time to pray. Others live at church, not at home. It's possible to overwork, even in Christian service, to the point where love, joy, and peace no longer exist in your frantic life.

Spend time with Jesus and let Him put His righteousness in you. Ask Him about your recreational activities, how to spend your money, how to study, and how much time to spend with your family, etc. Don't put money, energy, and time into anything unless you know it's God's will.

You're young. If you're at all success oriented, then be especially careful what you start doing. Are you *sure* it's what God wants you to be working on right now? If Christ isn't first, you'll become a slave to your project. And even if you keep it in perspective, you'll have to give up other things to complete it. Get God's direction for each undertaking so you don't waste any of your life.

✔ Rethinking the Situation

When Krista awoke from her dream, it was so vivid in her mind that it seemed nearly real. And she knew that Jesus wasn't really number one in her life. Because of that she was riding a roller coaster. She was always putting all her eggs in one basket, and then bumming-out when her hopes were shattered.

She knew that if she put Jesus first, He'd never disappoint her, never disappear, and never change. She picked up her Bible and began to read: "Jesus looked at him and loved him. 'One thing you lack,' he said, 'Go sell everything you have and give to the poor, and you will have treasure in heaven. Then come, follow me.' At this the man's face fell. He went away sad, because he had great wealth."

"Lord," Krista prayed silently. "I don't want to be like that young man. I want you to always be number one in my life."

☛ Putting the Truth Into Practice

Try drawing the wheel of your life, making long spokes for the things to which you give high priority and shorter ones for those less important to you. Include eating, sleeping, studying, working, prayer, Bible reading, church, witnessing, social life, sports, hobbies, relaxing, buying clothes, spending time with your family, etc. The amount of time and money you spend is a good indication as to where an activity stands on your list of priorities. Are there changes you must make to live a balanced life, completely under the control of Jesus?

Ask God what you should do about the longest and shortest spokes in your wheel.

CHAPTER 41

Who Put the Price Tag on You?

Marina was an only child. Her parents were divorced, and her mother worked outside the home. Lonely and often depressed, Marina found it hard to make friends. When Becky, who was a smiling, poised, and caring girl, invited her to the Terrific Teens party, Marina was delighted. As she listened to the talk, "Finding Real Love in Jesus," she knew that she needed to invite Jesus into her heart. When she did, she began to see why Becky could be so happy.

For the first time in her life, Marina met people who really cared about her—friends who'd listen to her problems. At school, she stuck to Becky like glue. Every day, she counted on her to listen to the unabridged version of her latest tragedy. Becky was usually very patient, but one morning she greeted Marina with a desperate look. "I can't listen to you today," she said abruptly. "I've got to spend every minute studying for a big Spanish test." And with that she rushed into the library.

Marina burst into tears. The fight she'd had with her mother last night was so terrible she *had* to talk to someone. How could Becky be so rude? Although Becky was extra nice the next day, giving a complete explanation of the urgency of her studying for the exam, Marina shunned her.

Because Marina lived only six blocks from the home of the youth pastor, Vance, and his wife Judy, she started stopping in daily after school. Because her mother often put in extra hours at the office, and did only microwave cooking, Marina couldn't resist hanging around the pastor's home until she was invited to stay for supper. Judy had a lot of compassion. She grew accustomed to fixing supper while listening to the reasons why Marina had had a hard day.

One afternoon, though, Judy answered the doorbell with a despairing plea, "Marina, please understand. I can't talk to you now. Vance is speaking at a church at 7:00, the baby's fussy, I haven't started supper, and I haven't done anything to my hair all day."

Marina was deeply hurt. She wanted someone to comfort her and tell her that getting a D on her geometry test wasn't the end of the world. Feeling rejected, she decided to find someone else to confide in.

When Marina talked to Faith after a Terrific Teens meeting, she was especially understanding. "All my Christian friends are letting me down," Marina complained. "I just don't know where to turn."

"Here's my telephone number," Faith offered. "If a problem arises, just give me a call."

Marina began calling Faith two or three times a day. When her father put a ten-minute limit on phone calls, Marina called five times a day—she needed more time to detail her difficulties.

One day, Faith's father answered the phone: "Marina," he said firmly, "I can't allow Faith to talk to you more than twice a week. Her grades are suffering, and I need to have the line free for important calls."

With that, Marina stopped attending Terrific Teens meetings.

▼ ▼ ▼ THIS WAY OUT ▼ ▼ ▼

🖝 Asking God to Meet Legitimate Needs

Dear God, teach me how to bring each problem to you. Thank you for never getting tired of listening to me. As I learn to trust you with each situation, I'll stop wearing other people out with my tales of woe. Make me so secure in you—receiving your love and Your affirmation—that I won't feel hurt every time people can't or won't meet my needs or desires. Show me how to be sensitive to the feelings and the requirements of others.

✔ Getting the Facts Straight

Seldom set foot in your neighbor's house—too much of you, and he will hate you (Proverbs 25:17).

Do nothing out of selfish ambition or vain conceit, but in humility consider others better than yourselves. Each of you should look not only to your own interests, but also to the interests of others (Philippians 2:3–4).

All of you, clothe yourselves with humility toward one another (1 Peter 5:5).

As Christians, we are to think of others before ourselves, and to get rid of the pride that treats people as pawns to be used for our own convenience. In practical terms, it means that you put yourself in the place of another and try to understand how he or she feels. You sense the mood of your friend, and forget your own agenda if you see that it's not appropriate at the moment.

Here are some rules for friendship: Don't make yourself a nuisance. Don't pressure people. Don't be a leech. Visiting too often, staying too long, or coming just at mealtime is not only poor manners, it's a bad testimony.

Whether you're like Marina or Becky, you need to know the root cause and the remedy for the I-have-worse-problems-than-anyone-else-so-please-give-me-all-your-time-and-sympathy-or-I'll-be-offended personality:

1. Such a person hasn't learned that as a child of God he or she has a kind heavenly Father who is *always* ready to listen, and who has miraculous power to answer prayer. All of us need to confide in friends at times, but it is important to talk to God *first*. The more we learn to see God as our loving heavenly Father who supplies every need—emotional, physical, and spiritual—the less necessity we will have for pouring out our hearts to others.

2. They haven't discovered their true value. Each individual is *worth* the blood of Jesus. Christ died for *you*, and the blood of

Jesus is worth more than the whole universe. God has put His price tag on you, and your value is so great that it can't even be estimated. The people who are easily hurt allow others to "steal" their value. Their line of reasoning goes like this: "She doesn't have time to talk to me, so I don't count"; "He didn't invite me to his birthday party, so I must be a nerd"; "She called me a jerk, so I guess that's what I am."

It's wrong to let anyone devalue your worth. If someone says they don't have time for you for a good reason, give them the benefit of the doubt. And remember, you have intrinsic and immeasurable value that no human insult can alter. Next time someone belittles you, try this answer: "That's your opinion, but Jesus thinks I'm worth so much He died for me."

Rethinking the Situation

Vance and Judy went to see Marina. When Vance asked her what was wrong she informed him, "Christians don't put into practice any of the love they preach about. That's why I've lost interest in coming to Terrific Teens."

"Marina," Judy ventured, "you once told me that your mother never stopped complaining long enough to listen to you. Is that right?"

"You got it," Marina replied. "She's lost all her friends because she does *nothing* but talk about her problems. Her boss even told her that he'd fire her if she didn't learn to be more pleasant. I'm sure my dad divorced her because of her attitude. I'd live with my stepmother if I could, but she doesn't want me."

"Marina," Judy said kindly, "we want to help you and to keep you from falling into the same pattern of behavior as your mother. Can't you see that once you found someone who would listen, you didn't know where to stop?"

"It's partially our fault," Vance put in. "We didn't really teach you that you should talk to God about each situation *before* consulting another person. You expected of us what only God can give—twenty-four-hour, seven-days-a-week service with a smile, and with answers that are never wrong."

"Becky and Faith and I haven't rejected you, Marina," Judy continued. "We love you. But no one can be expected to drop everything, anytime of the day or night, to talk endlessly about the same problems over and over. You need to learn how much God loves you, how to trust Him as your Father, and how much you're worth to Him. That's the only way you'll overcome your insecurity. You'll break the self-destructive pattern you're establishing. We'll help you. I know you haven't had supper with us for a long time, and I'd like to invite you for a steak dinner tomorrow night."

"Thank you!" replied Marina. "I'll be there."

☑ Putting the Truth Into Practice

Would a graph showing your self-esteem look like the stock market report on the nightly news?

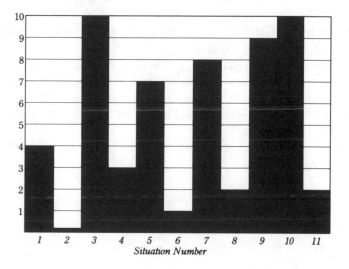

Situation Number

Situations

1. My sister said I was selfish.
2. Butch asked me if I got my haircut at the poodle shop.
3. Bill said I was cute.
4. I got a C on the exam.
5. My mother liked the new dress I bought.
6. Greg said he preferred redheads.
7. The teacher put my art project in the showcase.
8. A girl in gym class called me a klutz.
9. I wore the same kind of socks as the most popular girl in school.
10. Tom said hi to me in the hall.
11. My father said he wished my grades were as good as my sister's.

Make your own chart covering the events of the last two weeks. Keep in mind two things:

1. Letting others determine your value can become a great source of temptation. Often a teen will do anything for the approval of a certain member of the opposite sex—even if it's sin. Sometimes the desire for peer approval gets you into serious trouble.

2. It's ridiculous to give other people that much power over you. It's illogical that a comment from some insecure smart aleck should ruin your day. Why should a snippy girl who's stuck on herself snub you into oblivion?

Spend some uninterrupted quality time with God. As you read Luke 22, 23; Romans 5:8; Psalms 103; Jeremiah 31:3; Isaiah 43:4; and Deuteronomy 33:27, realize your true worth. And don't let anyone put you on the bargain table.

This doesn't mean that you ignore constructive criticism. On the contrary, the person who knows his or her true value in Christ can receive it graciously and ask God's help in making necessary changes. After all, every priceless diamond needs its rough edges polished so it can be even more beautiful.

Just make sure that it is God, and not another person, who puts the price tag on you.

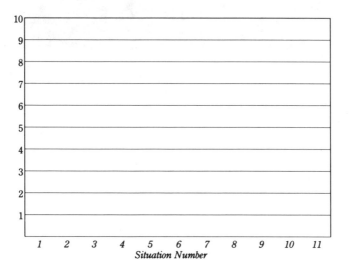

Situation Number

Situations

1. _____

2. _____

3. _____

4. _____

5. _____

6. _____

7. _____

8. _____

9. _____

10. _____

11. _____

CHAPTER 42

The Prodigal Son Returns

Kurt had a hard time during his growing up years. When he was six, his father left home for another woman.

Although Kurt knew his mother loved him, she was such a talented and efficient person that Kurt felt inferior, and he became an underachiever who found it easiest to let his mom do everything for him.

Kurt had a lot of memories of not being able to fit in anywhere. Christmas for him was very different from that of the kids whose parents sent greeting cards with photos of the whole family around the fireplace or the Christmas tree. Kurt traveled alone halfway across the country at Christmas time to stay with a stepmother who really didn't like him and a father who gave him presents instead of time. Other boys played on sports teams, went camping, and took swimming lessons, but Kurt's asthma kept him from fully participating. Short, and slightly built, he wondered if he'd ever grow to be a man.

At church he kept hearing that Jesus could take "bum raps" and turn them into something good. One night, when he was twelve, the sermon given by a special speaker made him see that he needed forgiveness for his bad attitude, and that he should give his life to Jesus.

But instead of accepting Christ that night, Kurt decided his problems were all God's fault. He grew more and more bitter.

Then a teacher explained, "Some people were born homosexuals. Don't worry if you think you are one."

Kurt wondered how he'd be able to tell if this were his problem. The fact that he thought all the girls in his class were ugly gave him some real concern.

Duane, his junior high Sunday school teacher, singled Kurt out for special attention. He even took him bowling and invited him to his home for supper. One day Duane told the class, "Don't ever believe that anyone is *born* a homosexual. The Bible tells us that all sexual expression between members of the same sex is sin. God doesn't plant any desire within the human heart without providing a healthy way for its expression.

"The problem is, the Devil is very good at using feelings, unfortunate experiences, and the lies of today's society to convince people that they *are* gay. If you or anybody you know struggles with this issue, I'd be more than happy to help you sort things out. God loves you and wants to heal the hurts that are causing your problems."

Kurt decided that his life was none of Duane's business. He resented his mother's authority and the fact that he was dependent on her. His rebellion at home kept his mother crying—and praying.

Desperate to be accepted, Kurt started running with a wild gang at school. Every time his mother tried to warn him, he exploded. When Duane took him out for supper and tried to get him to talk openly, Kurt only scoffed.

Since alcohol, drugs, and sex were in, Kurt decided to play the part. But his first attempt to use the backseat of a car with his girlfriend proved a disaster.

Now he was nearly convinced that he must be gay. The other guys bragged about their sexual conquests and seemed to be having the time of their lives.

It was then that Kurt met Herb, a man in his early thirties who was extremely wealthy. Herb's cynicism and sense of humor fascinated Kurt. He also seemed to be interested in him as a person and started buying him expensive gifts. When Kurt's mom objected, she received a barrage of verbal abuse.

Duane, who had faithfully kept in touch with Kurt, was also there to sound the alarm. But Kurt was not about to listen to anyone. He was sick of being told what to do at home and at school. He wanted to try something different.

When Duane's assessment that Herb wanted a homosexual partner proved accurate, Kurt didn't change his ways. Instead, he hung around with Herb and his gay friends, reading everything Herb gave him. Finally, he was convinced that he too was gay and that he should "come out of the closet."

Herb invited Kurt and a couple of other friends to go sailing in the Bahamas. It was the perfect chance to skip school, leave home and get away from it all. Kurt didn't want anyone to talk him out of it, so he left a note for his mom and just took off.

For a while his new life proved to be exciting. Herb gave him the attention he had never received from his father. But he still wasn't happy, and felt a deepening uneasiness. Then one night Herb got drunk and his secret slipped out. With glassy eyes and thick speech he mumbled, "This might be my last adventure. You see, I have AIDS."

▼ ▼ ▼ THIS WAY OUT ▼ ▼ ▼

☑ Asking God to Meet Legitimate Needs

Entering into a homosexual relationship (or any sexual relationship outside of marriage), is not a legitimate need, for you or anyone else. But behind the desire for this kind of sexual expression lie some real needs.

Let God himself fill your emotional longings. Permit Him to bring men and women into your life who can give you the healthy love and attention your parents, for whatever reason, have not been able to provide. And ask God to give you some good friends.

Never surrender to the idea that your feelings and emotions are there to guide you. A child may wish to eat chocolate all day long, but that doesn't mean it's good for him. You may think that avoiding work is pleasant, but in the end you'll pay for it. Stirrings within you that seem to be seeking a homosexual outlet do not mean that you're programmed for perversion anymore than falling in love with someone assures you that you've found your life's partner. The Devil very cleverly tries to make us think that our emotional reactions should determine our actions. Don't fall for his lies.

Dear God, my emotions are all mixed up right now. There are a lot of feelings inside me that I don't understand, especially feelings of _____ and _____ . Help me to realize that if I set my will toward obeying you, sooner or later my feelings will catch up with me. Thank you that you loved me enough to give me rules to live by.

✔ Getting the Facts Straight

A man who strays from the path of understanding comes to rest in the company of the dead (Proverbs 21:16).

He who obeys instructions guards his life, but he who is contemptuous of his ways will die (Proverbs 19:16).

Stern discipline awaits him who leaves the path; he who hates correction will die (Proverbs 15:10).

A man who remains stiff-necked after many rebukes will suddenly be destroyed—without remedy (Proverbs 29:1).

Satan's job is to deceive everyone into thinking that bad is good—and he puts in a lot of overtime! We're continually bombarded with his lies: Following the Ten Commandments is boring; If it feels good, do it; Freedom should have no limits; Some people are born homosexual; A marriage license is just an unnecessary piece of paper—and on and on.

Those who really seek God, and obey everything they know about His requirements, have some measure of immunity to Satan's deception. We read about it in Proverbs 4:18–19: "The path of the righteous is like the first gleam of dawn, shining ever brighter till the full light of day. But the way of the wicked is like deep darkness; they do not know what makes them stumble."

The things the Devil uses to tempt us differ according to the problems in our backgrounds, our personalities, and our circumstances. He will try to destroy one person through homosexuality, another through drugs, others through living together without being married, some through pride, and still others through false doctrine. While Kurt's story is *not* typical of every person who falls into homosexuality, it does illustrate a biblical principle: Disobedience to what you know God wants you to do sets you up to be deceived in some way by the Devil.

Realize that the more you ignore God's rules, the worse your spiritual vision becomes. Not only do you begin to believe things that are completely untrue, your words and your life-style teach the same untruths to others. It says in 1 Timothy 4:2 that false teachings "come through hypocritical liars, whose consciences have been seared as with a hot iron." The Scriptures also show us that disobedience to God is a prelude to the deception leading to sexual sin: "The mouth of an adulteress is a deep pit; he who is under the Lord's wrath will fall into it" (Proverbs 22:14).

DON'T USE THIS TEACHING TO JUDGE OTHERS. *Apply it to your own life!* Decide to obey God and avoid the dreadful consequences of falling into Satan's trap of deception. Each time you harden your heart, you endanger your spiritual life.

◤ Rethinking the Situation

Anger rose in Kurt. "You mean you *knew* you had AIDS and you didn't even tell me?" he agonized. "You're a murderer! And I'm your victim."

A full moon glistening on the tranquil sea contrasted sharply with the emotions Kurt felt raging within. Not only had he been deceived and used, but was possibly infected with a deadly virus. If only he'd listened! If only he'd lived by the truth he'd been taught. How could he ever face his mother? Maybe he should just jump overboard . . .

But then he thought of the story of the Prodigal Son. He pictured the flannelgraph figures his Sunday school teacher had placed on the board and remembered her words: *If you ever run away from the Lord like this boy did, don't forget that God has the heart of a Father and is waiting for you to return.*

Mentally, he replayed the youth retreat speaker's funny dramatization of the same story, ending with: "It doesn't matter what you did. If you truly repent, God will welcome you with open arms."

He also recalled the senior pastor's version of the parable, and the scripture he used to close his sermon: "I tell you that in the same way there will be more rejoicing in heaven over one sinner who repents than over ninety-nine righteous persons who do not need to repent" (Luke 15:7).

Tears filled Kurt's eyes as he cried out to God. He asked for forgiveness and surrendered what was left of his life to Jesus. And in spite of all the sins of the past and the uncertainties of the future, his heart was beginning to match the majestic stillness of the sea.

✔ Putting the Truth Into Practice

1. If you, like Kurt, are having any problems with your sexual identity, there is a place you can write to for information. Ministries that specialize in helping those struggling with homosexual feelings exist around the nation. For the address of the ministry nearest you, contact EXODUS INTERNATIONAL, P.O. Box 2121, San Rafael, California 94912, or phone (415) 454–1017.

2. Build some walls against deception that could occur in any area of your life. That means learning to accept correction and instruction so you can claim Proverbs 13:6, "Righteousness guards the man of integrity."

   a. List areas in your life where you constantly ignore or resist advice and correction. (Include even minor things like cleaning your room and choosing suitable clothes):

   _____

   _____

   _____

   _____

   _____ .

   b. List the areas in which God is trying to get through to you but you've been holding out (for instance: tithing, dedicating your life to full-time Christian service, etc.):

   _____

   _____

   _____

   _____

   _____ .

   Surrender these areas to God and let Him soften your heart. Don't let the Devil find an open door for his deception.

CHAPTER 43

And God Said, "He Who Hates Correction Is Stupid!"[1]

Drew was the kind of fellow who liked to get things done quickly. No grass grew under his feet! He was efficient, and impatient with those who couldn't keep up with him. Once he got his drivers license, he quickly earned the nickname, "Lightning." Although his friends were impressed, his father took a dim view of the situation.

One day, his father sat down with him to have a serious talk. "Drew," he warned, "the way you drive, you could easily kill someone. Every accident you have will raise our insurance—and *you're* going to have to pay the difference yourself. Being a Christian means being responsible in every area. You're a fine son, but behind the wheel you turn into a monster."

"Okay, okay," Drew mumbled halfheartedly. "I'll be more careful." But to himself, he thought, *My reflexes are a lot faster than Dad's, and I know what I'm doing.*

The day he drove his mother to the airport to pick up Aunt Karen turned out to be traumatic, to say the least. On the way out, his mom tried hard not to say anything, but when he cut into traffic, almost causing an accident, she screamed. For the next ten minutes she lectured Drew on his driving. But he was thinking about the big football game with Southwest, and tuned her out.

After picking up Aunt Karen's luggage, Drew was in a big hurry to get home in time for the game. Swerving in and out of traffic, his speedometer reading was ten miles over the speed limit.

"Drew," Aunt Karen pleaded, "please let me out. I'm just too nervous to ride with you."

Annoyed, Drew drove even more recklessly. Finally, when he

---

[1]Proverbs 12:1, NIV.

slammed on the brakes and slid into a busy intersection, Aunt Karen got out and hailed a passing cab.

His mother was mortified, and when they got home, Drew's father took the car keys away for three months.

For Drew, it was a terrible punishment, because he loved driving more than anything. He even dreamed of being a race car driver. But there was a big bright spot in those three months: Drew got to know Amber, a girl who was very sweet and caring. Since she lived across town, Drew spent hours on the bus—and she was worth it! He couldn't wait to have his car privileges again.

How proud he felt when he was finally able to pick up Amber in style and drive her to a nice restaurant. After a wonderful steak dinner and some delightful conversation, Amber's face became solemn. "Drew," she said seriously, "please promise me something."

"I'll promise *you* anything," he said, smiling.

"Don't drive so fast," she begged. "I'm almost afraid to ride with you."

Although this upset him, Drew said nothing, and tried to slow down for a while. But he intended to make Amber trust him so implicitly that she would realize what an expert driver he was.

One evening when Drew arrived to pick up Amber for a hockey game, she wasn't ready. She didn't seem to realize how important the state hockey championship was. The tickets were expensive, and Drew fidgeted and fumed as he waited. Amber rushed down the steps, repeating over and over how sorry she was. They were off.

By this time it was snowing heavily and visibility was poor. The woman driving ahead of Drew was proceeding down the freeway with snail-like precaution. They were late, after all, and Drew felt he had to change lanes. Glancing over his shoulder quickly, he gunned it—but he'd failed to see a fast-approaching little white sports car. There was a crunch of metal, the shattering of glass—and the sight of warm, red blood oozing from Drew's arm. After that, he blacked out.

THIS WAY OUT

Asking God to Meet Legitimate Needs

Receiving correction and instruction is a necessary part of a healthy Christian life. Not only should you accept it, you should ask for it. Seek the advice of men and women of faith.

Dear God, help me to accept constructive criticism. Make me willing to change when I'm wrong. Teach me to value the opinion of others. Show me the people who could give me godly advice.

Getting the Facts Straight

Whoever loves discipline loves knowledge, but he who hates correction is stupid (Proverbs 12:1).

He who ignores discipline comes to poverty and shame, but whoever heeds correction is honored (Proverbs 13:18).

He who listens to a life-giving rebuke will be at home among the wise. He who ignores discipline despises himself, but whoever heeds correction gains understanding (Proverbs 15:31–32).

A rebuke impresses a man of discernment more than a hundred lashes a fool (Proverbs 17:10).

Learning to accept constructive criticism is like driving down a middle lane between two extremes. On one side are the people who let criticism run their lives: If Robin doesn't like the sweater, it stays in the closet forever. If Uncle Carl doesn't praise the performance, depression sets in. The I've-got-to-please-everyone-or-it's-the-end-of-the-world kind of person lives in constant frustration. On the other side, you'll find those who've decided to automatically reject correction. Their missile system is all set up to retaliate the moment someone questions anything they do.

Here are some guidelines to help you remain teachable while avoiding extremes:

1. Maintain an if-that's-really-true-I'm-willing-to-change attitude.
2. Bring each criticism to God in prayer, asking Him if what the person said is correct.
3. Seek the counsel of a mature Christian who knows you well if you need advice on whether to ignore a statement or take it to heart.
4. Follow the Scriptures *no matter what anyone says*.
5. Be especially sensitive to doing something about changing the areas that several people have commented on.
6. If there are topics that no one can approach without your lashing out in self-defense, it's a sign that something is wrong. Prayerfully ask God for His help and guidance in getting to the root of the problem—and solving it.

✔ Rethinking the Situation

When Drew regained consciousness, he was in a hospital emergency room. At first he wasn't even sure what had happened. But he was well aware of the pain in his arm. By the time they wheeled him into a private room, his parents had arrived. "You're not that badly hurt," his mother comforted. "Your arm is broken, but it will mend."

Slowly his memory started working again, and he recalled that he and Amber had been on their way to the hockey game. "How is Amber?" he questioned. "Did she get hurt?"

The look on his mother's face frightened him. "She's in another section of the hospital. They're taking good care of her," she answered evasively. A nurse walked in, then, with some pain pills.

That night, Drew's sleep was fitful. He kept dreaming that his mother was telling him to slow down, but he'd speed up and crash into a cement wall. Then he'd start looking for Amber, who seemed to have disappeared. More than once he woke up screaming, *"Where is Amber? Where is Amber?"*

When he was released from the hospital Drew learned the truth. Amber lay unconscious in the intensive care unit. Her life was still in the balance.

Drew began sobbing. "It's all my fault. *My fault!* If only I'd listened to the complaints of my passengers." His horrible impatience and the pride in his driving ability might cost Amber her life. Tearfully he asked God and Amber's parents for forgiveness.

In a couple of weeks, Amber was strong enough to hear Drew say, "I'm sorry." As he watched her suffer, and realized how long the road to recovery would be, he decided that the next time someone offered him constructive criticism, he'd listen.

✔ Putting the Truth Into Practice

Fill in the chart on the next page.

1. Quickly check the items on your list for number four. Ask God if your faultfinders have hit on some real defects. Deal with anything that's true, and disregard the rest.
2. Seriously consider how you can make changes in areas covered by numbers two and three. Ask God to give you His method. If you suspect that a couple of these accusations are false, sound out a trusted Christian friend.
3. Make the topics in column one a matter of daily prayer, asking God to heal the wounds you're protecting. Seek the counsel of a mature Christian in dealing with these problems.
4. Remember! "It is a badge of honor to accept valid criticism."[2]

---

[2]James T. Draper, Jr., *Proverbs: Practical Directions for Living* (Wheaton, Ill.: Tyndale House Publishers, 1971), p. 126.

PUTTING THE TRUTH INTO ACTION

1. Topics that no one can touch without getting bombarded by my self-defense system.	2. Correction given by parents, teachers, bosses, youth pastors, and others in authority.	3. Areas of needed improvement which several people have called to my attention.	4. Criticism given by people who are always on my case and want to put me down.

CHAPTER 44

The Christian Life Isn't "Fit In, Weaklings and Marshmallows"

Ryan was tired of being considered weird.

"Don't you know any swear words?" Todd had asked him. "You talk like a little old lady."

"What do you mean you're saving sex for marriage?" Russ had scoffed. "You might not even live that long."

"Look who's sipping Coca-Cola," Danielle chirped to the cast of the play the night they went to Laura's house after the final perform- ance. "Ryan, we're all waiting for the day you'll grow up."

Somehow it didn't seem worth it to hold out any longer. Phil and Dusty both came from Christian homes, and *they* drank. Dusty's par- ents believed that total abstinence was legalistic, and served wine in their home. Ryan had heard too much about how drugs could destroy your mind to want to experiment in that area. But almost everyone drank—how could it be that bad? He longed to be totally accepted as "one of the guys."

When Josh invited his friends over after the game, Ryan tagged along. Not wanting to appear different, he drank right along with the rest. Although his conscience objected, his desire to fit in won out. He drank as much as they did. By the time he got home, he was so dizzy and sick he could hardly make it up the stairs. The next morning he felt awful.

But Monday at school the other guys went out of their way to welcome him as a full-fledged member of the group. And he did ap- preciate the sense of belonging. When Bruce announced a "kegger" at his house on Friday night, Ryan knew he'd be there. He decided getting sick was part of the package, and after a while he'd learn to tolerate liquor a little better.

Soon he learned that alcohol dulled his senses and helped him avoid stress, so he started drinking on the sly during the week. His grades began to drop, and he lost interest in church activities. Then his mom found some empty beer cans in his room.

His parents launched a crusade to reform him. But he only drank more, quarreling with his folks and even fighting with kids at school when he was under the influence of alcohol.

One night he arrived home in a police car. He'd been picked up for drunken driving. His parents laid it on the line: He wasn't going to be able to drive for six months.

That didn't bother him much, since his drinking buddies always picked him up.

When they changed classes at the end of the semester, he found himself sitting next to Rochelle in English class. She was really a sharp girl. Finally, Ryan got up enough courage to ask her out. Her answer really shook him up: "I wouldn't go anywhere with you. You're nothing but a drunk."

▼ ▼ ▼ THIS WAY OUT ▼ ▼ ▼

☑ Asking God to Meet Legitimate Needs

Although there is no verse in the Scriptures that says, "Thou shalt not touch a drop of alcohol," you really don't need to drink if you are fully dependent on Jesus for joy and freedom. Ephesians 5:18 suggests this great substitute for alcohol: "Do not get drunk on wine, which leads to debauchery (indulgence in sensual pleasure). Instead, be filled with the Spirit." That supernatural power of the Holy Spirit not only makes drinking unnecessary, but can strengthen you to the point that peer pressure won't dictate your decisions.

Dear God, fill me with so much of your power and love that I set the standards, instead of yielding to the standards of others. Give me Christian friends to hang around with who will help me to influence those around me, instead of being influenced by them. Thank you for answering this prayer.

☑ Getting the Facts Straight

Wine is a mocker and beer is a brawler; whoever is led astray by them is not wise (Proverbs 20:1).

Do not join those who drink too much wine or gorge themselves on meat (Proverbs 23:20).

It is not for kings . . . to drink wine, not for rulers to crave beer, lest they drink and forget what the law decrees, and deprive all the oppressed of their rights. Give beer to those who are perishing, wine to those who are in anguish; let them drink and forget their poverty and remember their misery no more (Proverbs 31:4–7).

Non-drinkers have fewer health problems, live longer, and are better insurance risks. The combination of alcohol and driving is the leading cause of death for people under age 25.[1]

Even today's permissive society protects minors by setting a legal drinking age. Yet more and more teenagers drink, and not without danger.

"Alcohol is the most used and abused drug in America today. . . . In 1987, the U.S. Secretary of Health and Human Services, Otis Bowen, said nearly five million adolescents have a drinking problem—that's three out of every 10!2" "The tragedy is that 50% of heavy drinkers in high school become alcoholics."[3]

Clearly, drinking involves risks. Yet people seem to choose to drink for two reasons: (1) To be accepted socially; (2) to "relax" and to escape. Proverbs tells us that alcoholic beverages are for losers

---

[1]Teenage Drinking (Weymouth, Mass.; Life Skills Education, 1988), p. 13.
[2]Ibid., p. 1.
[3]James T. Draper, Jr., *Proverbs: Practical Devotions for Living* (Wheaton, Ill.: Tyndale House Publishers, Inc., 1971), p. 104.

who have no hope—a drug of choice for those who wish to ride second class. But drinking does not belong in the life of the person who has set his or her sights on higher things.

True, it's not a mortal sin to take a drink. But that's not the issue: It's making the wisest and best choice. Christians who learn to receive all that God has to give them through the power of the Holy Spirit don't need to depend on any artificial high. They can turn to a loving and all-powerful God instead of a bottle when they've had a bad day. Love, joy, and peace are available in inexhaustible supply to those who wait upon the Lord. A victorious Christian just doesn't need a drink.

A Christian can never conform to the world and still maintain his or her testimony. Even if you did some social drinking you'd still stand out. God says, "Therefore come out from them and be separate, says the Lord. Touch no unclean thing, and I will receive you" (2 Corinthians 6:17).

Whether or not to drink is just one of the many options that involve choosing between the mediocre and the best. Once you decide to stop straddling the fence and to rely on God's power to be different, you'll find each choice a lot easier. The Holy Spirit can supply you with the enthusiasm and the energy to enjoy swimming upstream. Besides, the Christian life isn't "Fit In, Weaklings and Marshmallows"—it's "Onward Christian Soldiers!"

☑ Rethinking the Situation

What Rochelle said took Ryan by surprise. She wasn't even a Christian. She went to the parties he attended, and she even drank. Yet she had called him a *drunk*! The next day he got his report card—four D's and an F. And he'd always been an honor-roll student.

Ryan realized it was time to come back to God. Only now he was going to follow Jesus without any compromise. He asked the Lord for forgiveness, emptied the cans of beer he'd hidden in the garage, and got out his Bible. Every day he prayed for strength, and God rewarded his faith. He stepped out of the fog into a beautiful world full of challenges and adventure. His relationship with his parents and his teachers improved dramatically.

And Holly, a pretty girl from church, seemed very pleased with the extra attention he was giving her.

254

☑ Putting the Truth Into Practice

Here is a list of things you can do to avoid feeling forced into drinking. Check the things you are already doing and decide to implement at least two of the others.

_____ 1. Hang around with kids who don't drink.

_____ 2. Go to Jesus *first* when your feelings are hurt or you've had a bad day.

_____ 3. Pray for more Christian friends at school.

_____ 4. Study and apply to your life what the Bible teaches about the power of the Holy Spirit.

_____ 5. List all the negative features of drinking—even get some facts about alcohol from the library.

_____ 6. Find out how an ex-alcoholic views drinking.

_____ 7. Spend time with Jesus every day praying for the courage to be different.

CHAPTER 45

My Mind's Made Up—Don't Confuse Me With the Facts!

Jessica couldn't believe the day had finally arrived—the day for which their high school band had practiced so much and worked so hard. It was a dream come true! They watched as their instruments and luggage were packed away in two big chartered buses. Waving goodbye to their families and friends, they settled back for the long ride to Pasadena. The Fairview High School band was going to play at the Rose Bowl!

As they passed through a neighboring town, Jessica relived the events that had made this trip possible. Mr. Doyle, the energetic and talented young band director, had transformed the music department. His enthusiasm was contagious. When he first mentioned the Rose Bowl, everyone thought it was impossible. But extra practices, bake sales, car washes, selling Florida oranges, and many other fund raising projects had made this dream a reality.

But there was one thing that made Jessica a little uneasy. She was a Christian and had some good close friends who shared her faith and her standards—but none of them were in the band. The four-girls-in-a-hotel-room policy had placed her with Emily, Melissa, and Jamie, three girls she considered rather wild. Also, Mr. Kaminsky and his wife, who always chaperoned school trips and ran a tight ship, had to stay behind because of a death in the family. They had been replaced by Ms. Vaughn and Mr. Lewis, new teachers who were lax on discipline. She was glad that Trevor, a guy from her church, was also in the band.

Because they didn't have any extra money, they drove straight through, making as few stops as possible. After forty-eight hours on the road with lots of noise and little sleep, they arrived at their hotel completely exhausted. No one even objected when Mr. Doyle said everyone was to be in bed by 8:00. Besides, they had to be down in the lobby dressed in their band uniforms by 7:00 the next morning.

Because they were to be the first high school band in the parade, they would be able to watch the rest of it. When Jessica got close to the first float, she squealed with delight. She'd never seen so many flowers in her life! She wondered how many people would be watching on television and what the announcer would say about the Fairview High School Band.

As the drummers began the cadence, they all lined up. Butterflies filled Jessica's stomach as she tried to remember everything. "Keep those lines straight. Don't you dare get out of step. The first note is the most important, so *hit* it!"

It was a long parade, but everyone was much too excited to be tired. When they finished, Mr. Doyle congratulated them. "Good job troops! Now, everyone stay in this area and watch the parade. Find something to eat, and the buses will be back at 1:00 to take you to the game." Uncomfortable around the other girls, Jessica found a place to sit down and admire the flowered floats. Then she walked around a little until the bus came.

As the students boarded the bus, it was obvious that most of them had been drinking. Ms. Vaughn and Mr. Lewis had disappeared, and Mr. Doyle had gone to pick up the trophy they'd won. The bus drivers had other assignments, so they took off—even though several people were missing. Students passed around cans of beer and continued drinking at the game.

That was when Melissa became loud and obnoxious. She approached Chuck, who was so stoned he was like a zombie. "I like you. Come up to my hotel room tonight—number 212."

Jessica was shocked, but Chuck didn't even seem to hear her. Tony had passed out and Pat, who was usually painfully shy, had become so belligerent that he and Curt were on the verge of a fist fight.

Hoping she could somehow escape and sit by someone sober, Jessica spied Trevor—but he also had a can of beer in his hands!

Just then Mr. Doyle appeared. Angry, he confiscated all the beer and liquor.

Jessica was one of the few who showed up for the buffet supper the hotel had planned for the band. That night her roommates were sick, so she got very little sleep.

Wow! she thought, as she stared into the darkness, *I never knew what I was missing by not drinking—all kinds of horrible things.*

THIS WAY OUT

☑ Asking God to Meet Legitimate Needs

Dear God, I thank you that you are the source of peace. Teach me to trust you with each day so I can live a relaxed life. I know it's not your will that I depend on a bottle or a chemical to dull my senses so I can forget my problems. Instead, give me your stability so I can face them and solve them. Right now _____ _____ is bothering me. I put the situation completely in your hands and will exchange this burden for your peace.

☑ Getting the Facts Straight

For drunkards and gluttons become poor, and drowsiness clothes them in rags (Proverbs 23:21).

Who has woe? Who has sorrow? Who has strife? Who has complaints? Who has needless bruises? Who has bloodshot eyes? Those who linger over wine who go to sample bowls of mixed wine. Do not gaze at wine when it is red, when it sparkles in the cup, when it goes down smoothly! In the end it bites like a snake and poisons like a viper. Your eyes will see strange sights and your mind imagine confusing things. You will be like one sleeping on the high seas, lying on top of the rigging. "They hit me," you will say, "But I'm not hurt! They beat me, but I don't feel it! When will I wake up, so I can find another drink?" (Proverbs 23:29–35).

The consequences of excessive drinking are pretty terrible—and Proverbs 23 gives us a graphic description. Inability to carry out responsibility results in financial problems. An alcoholic finds himself/herself in constant conflict with those who in some way depend on them. Money is wasted, foolish decisions are made, work is faulty or left undone, and so the list goes on. And it's very easy for the drinker to shift the blame and become a complainer.

Accidents and fights can cause needless bruises, and there are hangovers and general health problems. The mental confusion not only causes one to make a fool of himself, but sometimes there are frightening hallucinations. Senses are dulled to the point that a person under the influence of alcohol has a false courage that flirts with danger. The drunkard may not feel pain, but he also misses out on the delights of life. And worst of all, the only real desire of such a person is looking for the next drink.

A picture such as this should make you leery of drinking. So should the fact that "the most sophisticated part of the brain—the part that controls judgment—is the first affected by alcohol."[1] Yet there seems to be a pride in all of us that makes us think that we're exempt from the risks that jeopardize others. The I'm-so-special-that-I-can-play-with-fire-without-getting-burned attitude seems to be a universal malady. And it's straight from the pit. Pride comes before destruction just as surely as it snows in Alaska in winter.

"He's not a Christian, but I'll marry him and then win him to Christ"; "Don't tell me how to act on a date. I have plenty of self-control"; "It's okay for *me* to drink, because *I* know when to quit." If statements like these reveal your Superman or Wonder Woman complex, watch out! God gave a very special warning to those who "linger over wine." You ignore it at your own risk.

☞ Rethinking the Situation

The first day of the bus ride home things were pretty quiet. But twenty-four hours later, kids were laughing and joking and goofing around.

"After the parade we really had a blast," Melissa was saying. "Too bad our chaperons are back, or we could have another 'kegger' right here on the bus."

---

[1] Teenage Drinking, (Weymouth, Mass.: Life Skills Education, 1988), p. 3.

"Yeah," Emily responded. "There's nothing like a little booze to loosen you up."

Jessica could hardly believe her ears. Didn't they even remember being sick all night? Wasn't Melissa embarrassed about the things she'd said? They seemed to have no regrets about the beautiful scenery and gorgeous sunset they'd missed.

Just then, Trevor plopped down in the empty seat beside Jessica. They talked about the trip and began discussing what had happened at the game. "Trevor," Jessica chose her words carefully. "I was surprised to see you drinking, too."

"I didn't get *drunk*, did I?" he defended. "The Bible only says you shouldn't get drunk. It doesn't say you can't drink a drop."

"I know," responded Jessica. "It's just that after what I saw, I want to stay miles away from any liquor. I want to serve Jesus without impaired judgment and without leaving a bad example for those younger than me to follow."

Trevor shrugged. "*I* can drink, because *I* know when to stop."

After Trevor left to go back and sit with the guys, Jessica looked out the window at the rolling hills. There was an arrogance in Trevor's attitude that frightened her. How could he be so blind to something so obviously dangerous? And for the first time in her life she realized the depth of meaning in the Bible verse she had learned as a child: "Wine is a mocker and beer a brawler; whoever is led astray by them is not wise" (Proverbs 20:1).

▶ Putting the Truth Into Practice

I know a pastor who says this: "The *issue* isn't nearly as important as the *attitude* of your heart." It's pride and stubbornness that cause disaster. There is a test for determining if the Devil has deceived you at some point. When you've swallowed Satan's lies concerning some questionable activity, you'll adopt an I-know-what-I'm-doing, my-mind's-made-up-don't-confuse-me-with-the-facts mentality. If you're unwilling to take advice or change, WATCH OUT.

Pray, and ask the Lord to show you if you're hardening your heart in some area. If so, repent and start listening to God and to the advice of others.

CHAPTER 46

You Become Like the gods or the God You Believe In

Karlene and Audrey had hung around together since seventh grade. Karlene was a natural leader, and Audrey looked up to her.

Because Audrey's parents believed that she had the right to make her own choices, she was free to attend all the church events that Karlene invited her to. She went to Bible camp, youth activities and even to prayer meeting. Although Karlene noticed that Audrey could be easily influenced, she had no doubt that Audrey was a Christian—that is, until Jodi appeared on the scene.

Likeable, dynamic, and extremely pretty, Jodi caused a sensation wherever she went. When she started attending mind control seminars, they immediately became popular. Although Karlene warned Audrey and pleaded with her not to sign up, she went anyway.

Soon Audrey had changed her entire belief system—and had stopped going to church or reading the Bible. "There's good in *all* religions," she informed Karlene. "Each person needs to experiment and find out what brings them the most satisfaction. I like some things at your church, but I could never be restricted to such a narrow choice."

"But *all* religions can't be true," Karlene argued. "They teach contradictory things."

"What's true for you may not be true for me," Audrey responded easily. "But that's no big deal. I'll just go with whatever works for me."

Karlene realized that reasoning with Audrey was useless.

As the year went on, Karlene saw Audrey change completely. A girl with impeccable moral standards, she decided to sleep with her boyfriend. When Karlene tried to talk her out of it, her only answer was, "There are many sacred writings in the world, and I prefer not to accept all the biblical taboos."

Soon, Audrey was talking about conversations with spirit beings and evolving into another sphere of consciousness. Formerly an honor roll student, she now felt studying was a waste of time. "Besides," she told everyone, "my teachers are still bound by the physical universe—and I'm transcending above it."

But that wasn't all. When Audrey's boyfriend broke up with her, she went after any guy she could get—and many of them were a lot older than her. It was as if passion ruled her life. She also started doing drugs, and her personality became so different that Karlene felt like she hardly knew her. Then, finding herself pregnant, Audrey had an abortion without hesitation.

But when Tony heard about it, his blood boiled because he assumed the child was his. To him, abortion was the unpardonable sin. He got drunk and came over to Audrey's house with a pistol in his pocket. They ended up screaming at each other, and Tony started shooting. He hit Audrey in the hip.

"She killed my kid," Tony told police later. "She committed murder."

▼ ▼ ▼ THIS WAY OUT ▼ ▼ ▼

✒ Asking God to Meet Legitimate Needs

God has already given you something that you can't live happily without—definite rules to follow. You only need to be in constant contact with Him in order to receive the motivation and the power to obey His commands.

Dear God, I am tempted sometimes to think that _____ *is okay, even though your Word says it isn't. Keep me so close to you that I won't even consider the ideas of other life philosophies.*

✔️ Getting the Facts Straight

Where there is no revelation, the people cast off restraint; but blessed is he who keeps the law (Proverbs 29:18).

Every word of God is flawless; he is a shield to those who take refuge in him. Do not add to his words, or he will rebuke you and prove you a liar (Proverbs 30:5–6).

For these commands are a lamp, this teaching is a light, and the corrections of discipline are the way to life (Proverbs 6:23).

Your word is a lamp to my feet and a light for my path (Psalm 119:105).

My people are destroyed from lack of knowledge . . . because you have ignored the law of your God (Hosea 4:6).

A high school girl once explained her new non-Christian philosophy to me, adding, "But don't worry, my ideas are different but my conduct will remain the same."

I answered, "No, you'll change your actions to conform to your beliefs."

Long after I'd forgotten what I'd said, she returned to tell me that my "prophecy" had come true.

It wasn't *my* prediction—it's a biblical principle: "Where there is no revelation (which, according to a commentary, could also be translated as *God's guidance or authority*), the people cast off restraint."[1] In the life of a person who doesn't believe in the rules set down by the God who created the universe, anything goes. People really do become like the gods or the God they worship.

There are several ways to get yourself into the position of breaking through the barriers that God has designed for your protection. You can throw the Bible overboard like Audrey did, fall for a philosophy that has no absolutes, and run wild. It's also possible for you to add

---

[1]Irving L. Jensen, *Everyman's Bible Commentary: Proverbs* (Chicago: Moody Press, 1980), p. 33.

or subtract something from God's Word in a couple places, so that you won't feel guilty about your sin. Or you can simply ignore the Scriptures and gradually fall into deception.

The *smart* option is to hang on to everything the Bible says. As you act in accordance with the fact that "every word of God is flawless," you'll find that God is a "refuge to those who take refuge in Him."

Because you live in a society that has rejected obedience to God's commands, a culture that's chosen unlimited freedom, it's especially important that you take Bible study seriously. Unless you cling to the Scriptures and obey them, you'll be swept along with the tide of confusion and lawlessness.

✒ Rethinking the Situation

Karlene and the whole youth group had been praying for Audrey. They took turns visiting her in the hospital. At first, when they tried to talk to her about Jesus, she wasn't interested. But as surgery and several complications prolonged her hospital stay, the only people who continued to faithfully visit her were the Christians.

One Saturday afternoon, Karlene stopped by the hospital. Audrey had been crying. "What's wrong?" Karlene asked.

"Everything," replied Audrey. "Everything! Not one of the guys who told me that they loved me has come to see me. Tony could have at least apologized for trying to kill me! But before he shot me, he kept screaming, 'You killed my baby! You killed my baby!' I don't understand. Everybody gets abortions—except Christians. I'm so mixed up. I don't know what to do."

"If you decide to pick and choose, and make up your own standards, you become your own god," explained Karlene. "When I think of how fickle I can be, how often I change my mind, and all my emotional ups and downs, I'm glad that I trust in Jesus, who's the same yesterday, today, and forever. When I think of *all* the choices there are in the world, I'm thankful for God's guidelines because they protect me from danger."

"I envy you," Audrey admitted. "But I just can't believe that only one religion is right. I do want to know Jesus like you know Him, but I'm so confused."

Karlene started praying—and as she prayed, she was aware of a tremendous spiritual battle. Just then the pastor and his wife slipped silently into the room. They joined in asking God to clear Audrey's mind of all evil influences and satanic lies.

After a while, Audrey interrupted them, "I asked Jesus into my life, and I know He heard me!" she exclaimed. "Now the things you've been telling me make sense."

✔ Putting the Truth Into Practice

David affirmed: "Oh, how I love your law! I meditate on it all day long" (Psalm 119:97).

"I run in the path of your commands, for you have set my heart free" (Psalm 119:32).

"I will hasten and not delay to obey your commands" (Psalm 119:60).

Can you honestly say these things about *all* of God's commandments? If not, list the biblical rules you have trouble with: _____

_____

_____

_____

Pray that the Lord will bring you to the point that you *love* these laws. And remember, all of God's restrictions are made to protect you.

Self-Examination

Part V: Tips for Teens—Variety Pack

1. Which things are true about cherished dreams? _____
   a. Desiring something that is not God's will for your life can open the door to strong temptation.
   b. You should wipe out desire completely.
   c. Creativity and the ability to plan for the future are gifts from God.
   d. You need to submit your dreams to God and let Him judge their worth.
2. Which are secrets of a happy heart? _____
   a. Grinning and bearing it.

266

b. Constantly believing everything Jesus said.
c. Putting into practice the principles of trust and praise.
d. Learning to be grateful in all circumstances.
3. What things are *not* among the things that God prizes most? _____
   a. Consideration for others and a heart for God.
   b. Brains and beauty.
   c. A gentle spirit and purity.
   d. Sincerity and goodness.
4. What are some basic problems of the person who is easily offended?_____
   a. He/she allows the comments and actions of others to determine his/her self-worth.
   b. There is an inability to put oneself in the place of another.
   c. There isn't a complete dependence upon God our heavenly Father who is on duty twenty-four hours a day.
   d. He/she doesn't give a busy friend the benefit of the doubt.
5. *Never* surrender to the idea that your feelings and emotions are _____ .
6. _____ to what you know God wants you to do sets you up to be deceived in some way by the Devil.
7. He who hates correction is _____ (Proverbs 12:1).
8. Basically, Proverbs tells us that alcoholic beverages are for _____ .
9. Why is a cocky attitude so dangerous? _____
   a. Pride comes before destruction.
   b. You're not so special that you can play with fire and not get burned.
   c. "God opposes the proud but gives grace to the humble."
   d. It's the unpardonable sin.
10. You'll change your actions to conform to your _____ .

CHAPTER 47

Don't Sign Up for the Casualty List

ENLIST TODAY

Kent grew up in a Christian home, and as a teenager he was challenged by his pastor to do everything possible to search out God's wisdom. He decided to go for it. Praying constantly for wisdom, he studied his Bible diligently. He memorized scriptures and became a leader in his youth group. Many people profited from his wise and godly advice.

At college, Kent was active in student evangelism and discipling new Christians.

Graduating with honors, he studied law. Later, determined to make the world a better place, he ran for state representative.

Although his jealous older brother filed for the same office just to embarrass him, Kent's wisdom in handling the situation won him the election. Intelligent and full of workable new ideas, Kent became very popular with everyone. His dedication to high moral principles and his idealism introduced a breath of fresh air to the murky world of politics.

Everything was going his way, and the people at church still saw the same humble Christian commitment that Kent had always displayed. But Kent couldn't help noticing Cassandra, the brightest secretary in the state office building. Attractive as a model, enchanting, and witty, she seemed to always be around when Kent needed something. Although he cautioned others never to date a non-Christian, there was a praise concert he wanted Cassandra to hear.

After that, Kent decided she was so beautiful and sweet he just couldn't stay away from her. Soon he was hopelessly in love, and even though he knew it was wrong, he decided to marry her.

At first, Cassandra attended church with him, and there was no noticeable change in Kent's life. He was chosen as chairman of the building program, and under his able leadership an impressive sanctuary was erected. But within five years, Cassandra left Kent for a richer man.

Instead of repenting and seeking God, Kent started dating Anna, another knockout. Because Anna didn't believe in marriage, they simply had a private affair. Politically, his star was still rising, and Kent soon found himself in Washington, D.C.

Initially, he was shocked at the corruption and dishonesty. But after a while he learned to pad his expense account, accept gifts from lobbyists, and to use his power to gain personal advantage. Serving the people, guarding the taxpayer's money, and maintaining Christian principles in politics no longer seemed important.

When the romance between Kent and Anna faded, he married Tyne. She was a New-Ager, and he began meditating with her. But when their relationship became strained, they divorced.

Kent found yet another lover—a woman heavily involved in the occult. Because of her influence, he launched a bill that would tax the property of all Christian churches!

Finally, he lost his magic—and for the first time in twenty years Kent faced tough competition in an election. The public was beginning to distrust the "knight in shining armor" whom they'd first sent to the nation's capital. Somehow during his stay in Washington he had become a very rich man. His opponent was a Christian, but Kent used all the dirty tricks of politics to defeat him.

Actually, you've just read a true story—only the names and the particular time in history have been changed to protect the *guilty*! Except for presenting the facts in modern guise, this account accurately describes the rise and fall of a famous Biblical character. Who is he? _____

If you guessed Solomon, you're absolutely right! The success to failure story is that of King Solomon.

After his father died and he became king, Solomon wanted to follow God and lead His people well. He gave the brother who tried to steal the throne from him a fair shake. When God appeared to him in a dream with a fantastic offer: "Ask for whatever you want me to give you," Solomon didn't opt for a gorgeous wife or a mountain of money. He only wanted God's wisdom so he could rule fairly. But the Lord threw in a lot of extras because He was pleased with Solomon.

And Solomon really listened to God—closely enough to let the Holy Spirit use him to author most of the book of Proverbs. He built God's temple, and his dedication prayer indicates that he was accustomed to talking with God. And the Lord showed His favor by filling the whole place with His glory.

But Solomon, with all his knowledge of God and all the talents and special gifts the Lord had given him, chose to go his own way. In 1 Kings 11:9 we find a description of the situation: "The Lord became angry with Solomon because his heart had turned away from the Lord, the God of Israel, who had appeared to him twice." And if anyone knew better, it was Solomon!

Yet it all started—like the downfall of many a teenager—because Solomon wanted to be like everyone else. In his case, "everyone else" included the kings of the nations around Israel. Deuteronomy 17 lists three no-no's for Israelite kings: 1. They were not to acquire great numbers of horses; 2. They were not to take many wives; 3. They were not to accumulate large amounts of silver and gold. Solomon disregarded all three commands. As you will see, Solomon's problem all boils down to depending on something other than God for a sense of security and significance—a sin that we can easily fall into also if we're not careful.

Kings trusted in military force to keep their territories safe from invasion. In those days armies were made up of horses and chariots, and Solomon owned 1,400 chariots and 12,000 horses. Putting his total confidence in God seemed too old-fashioned.

Instead of praying for protection, he made a lot of peace treaties. That doesn't sound so bad, until you realize that in those days a peace treaty came complete with a wife! It was thought that an intermarriage between two royal families was the best guarantee against war. Solomon ended up with 700 wives of royal blood. Mistreating any of them could provoke attack. Certainly it would be risky to prohibit them from practicing their false religions. But Solomon found out that he loved having a harem, and he even worshiped with many of his wives. And he didn't stop at political convenience—he had 300 concubines of his own choosing.

Next, Solomon started a gold collection. Yearly he received *twenty-five tons* of gold—presumably from tribute and taxes. This didn't include wealth brought in through trade. And we do know that one such expedition came back with seventeen tons worth!

Because of the complaint people made to Solomon's son Rehoboam: "Your father put a heavy yoke on us," it is safe to assume that the common people sacrificed so that Solomon could have his gold goblets, the most elaborate throne in the world, and 500 shields of hammered gold, just for decoration. We're even told that "all the household articles in the Palace of the Forest of Lebanon were pure gold." Even his great accomplishment—the building of the temple—is offset by his erecting a bigger palace for himself, which took thirteen years to build. His respect for the things of God diminished to the point that he tried to kill Jereboam, whom the Lord's prophet had anointed to be the next king.

Solomon had fallen for the Devil's line: "Of course, you must be like all the other kings." Included in that package were power, sex, and wealth, the Devil's all-time best-sellers!

BUT WATCH OUT! Solomon's terrible decline all started with a simple decision: "I must copy what those around me are saying and doing, even if it violates the Scriptures." Any time you allow that kind of "hole in the dike," you risk terrible losses.

You can read the book of Proverbs a hundred times and work at putting it all into practice. But the day you say, "I know the Bible says it's bad, but everybody's doing it and I can't be different," you're opening yourself up for *Solomon's Syndrome.*

It happens more often than we'd like to think. One day, my Sunday school teacher came to class somewhat bummed-out. He'd run into the man who'd been his role model and dedicated Bible study teacher when he was in college. Now this man no longer believed in God and had divorced his wife.

So many start out well and then completely miss the mark. But you don't have to sign up on the casualty list!

There are those who stick to the Scriptures throughout their lives and permit God to fulfill His purposes for them. I read an article in a recent secular publication that concluded that, although many national Christian leaders had fallen, Billy Graham had maintained his integrity and was universally respected. A main reason for this, according to the writer, was that his career was marked with right decisions. In my opinion, there's a strong connection between Billy Graham's success and the great emphasis he puts on studying and practicing the book of Proverbs.

This is the testimony of Billy Graham: "For a number of years, I have made it a practice to read five psalms and one chapter of Proverbs a day. The Psalms teach us how to get along with God, and the Proverbs teach us how to get along with our fellowmen. . . . You cannot imagine the blessing this encounter with the Scriptures has been in my life, especially in recent years."[1]

Take the advice of James 1:22: "Do not merely listen to the word, and so deceive yourselves. Do what it says." Only then will you be able to look back on your life with no regrets.

Isn't that what you want?

---

[1]Irving L. Jensen, *Proverbs*, (Chicago: Moody Press, 1982), p. 33.

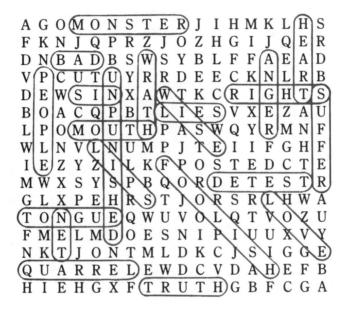

```
A G O (M O N S T E R) J I H M K L (H) S
F K N J Q P R Z J O Z H G I J Q (E) R
D N (B A D) B S (W) S Y B L F F (A) E A D
V (P) C U T U) Y R R D E E C K N (L) R B
D E (W) S I N) X A (W) T K C (R I G H T) S
B O A C Q P B T (L I E S) V X E Z A U
L P O (M O U T H) P A S W Q Y (R) M N F
W L N V (L N U M P J T E) I I F G H F
I (E) Z Y Z I L K (F) P O S T E D C T E
M W X S Y (S) P B Q O R (D E T E S T) R
G L X P E H R S) T J O R S R (L) H W A
(T O N G U E) Q W U V O L Q T V O Z U
F M (E) L M D) O E S N I P I U U X V Y
N K (T) J O N T M L D K C J S I G G E)
(Q U A R R E L) E W D C V D A H) E F B
H I E H G X F (T R U T H) G B F C G A
```

Answers to puzzle on page 153.